DARK SIDE
PHILOSOPHY

by

THE DARK LORDS

THE NINE ECHELONS OF SITH MASTERY, BOOK #4

Copyright © 2018 by The Dark Lords, Inc.

Printed in the United States of America

ISBN-13: 978-1727541045

First Edition, Imperial Year 8 (September 2018)

All rights reserved. This book or any portion thereof may not be reproduced or used in any manner whatsoever without the express written permission of the publisher except for the use of brief quotations in a book review. Anyone violating these conditions will be subject not only to legal action, but to black magickal attack by the Dark Lords and the wrath of the Dark Side of the Force!

Sith Academy Publications
sithacademy.com

CONTENTS

INTRODUCTION 5
GENERAL CONSIDERATIONS 7
    First Principles 9
    Dark Side Philosophy 14
    Light Side Philosophy 16
PHILOSOPHY OF POWER, EVIL AND WAR 21
    Power 21
    Evil 25
    War 31
METAPHYSICS 37
    Building Blocks of Reality 37
    Black Sunnite Metaphysics 43
    The Two Worlds 49
PHILOSOPHY OF DEATH 53
    Learning How to Die 53
    More Perspectives on Death 56
PHILOSOPHY OF HISTORY, POLITICS AND EMPIRE 69
    Philosophy of History 69
    Magick and Empire 73
    Ruling Systems 77
    Fascism 83
COSMIC PHILOSOPHY 88
    The Four Cosmic Schools 88
    Cosmism 89
    Acosmism 96
    Anti-Cosmism 99
    Cosmicism 102

Aspects of Sithism 107
- The Sith Code 107
- Aspects of Sithism 110
- Sith Spirituality 115

The Nine Pillars of Sithism 123
- The Primacy of Power 124
- The Tao of Darwin 125
- The Force and the Source 127
- The Power of the Dark Side 128
- The Superman 130
- Mind Power 136
- Multiversalism 138
- Galactic Empire 140
- Formlessness 141

A Survey of Philosophy 144
- Key Philosophies 144
- Recommended Reading 154

Echelon Four Doctrine 157
- Echelon Four Precepts 157
- Philosophy Quotes 159
- Philosophy Praxis 162
- Echelon Four Challenges 165

Epilogue 168

Correspondence 169

INTRODUCTION

This book is an investigation into the "Dark Side" philosophies that inform our project of empire, endarkenment and empowerment. It is the result of many years of reflection, action and study in darker realms of thought which most intellectuals are inclined to avoid.

The Dark Side path is not a way of abstract philosophizing that seeks some "ultimate truth", but of *weaponized thought* that seeks *unlimited power*. For philosophy, like every other animal trait or human tool, whether it be fangs, fire or firearms, language, ritual or religion, must prove its worth in a predatory, might-is-right, survival-of-the-fittest world. We take this as axiomatic in our black magickal *bor-zovrâd (dark philosophy)*. We are therefore going to ignore the main currents of "Light Side" Western philosophy, from Socrates and Jesus to Descartes, Locke, Kant and Hegel—which to our kind are a lineage of erroneous and insipid abstractions that have blinded beings to the power of the Dark Side and the shadow-mind for centuries. We are instead going to delve deeper and think outside the boxes of conventional Western thought to find philosophies that are suitably sharp-edged for our kind. Nietzsche spoke of philosophizing with hammers; our kind philosophize with sabers.

In truth our intellectual project is anti-philosophy, as philosophy is in our view a failed enterprise and an enterprise of failure. To manifest our Empire, we must in effect "kill all the philosophers". Everything that stands in the way of our greatness, darkness, power and conquest, that elevates some insipid quest for "truth", "justice" or "reason" above all other ideals, must be swept aside by bold thinkers whose imaginations and wills are unfettered by such feeble abstractions.

In this book we discuss the key thinkers and ideas that have influenced the development of our path of *Sithism*. It is not a work of systematic philosophy, but a collection of thoughts, essays and observations on many relevant topics. This will be a wide-ranging book, touching on all aspects of our worldview, metaphysics, morality, ideology, politics and way of life. It will be the most purely intellectual book in this series, dealing as it does with theories and ideals more than praxis, sorcery, warfare or political machinations, but it should be useful to those who value such thought.

Not every Dark Lord must be a philosopher, but one of the qualities that separates our kind from small-time sorcerers and gangsters is the possession of a well-developed philosophy. The Dark Lord respects the power of thought and is motivated by ideas. He can more than hold his own in any discussion of metaphysics, mythology or morality. He is not impressed by credentialed intellectuals who wave their "good-guy badges" at him or employ academic jargon in an effort to assert power over him. Nor is he abashed in the slightest by guilt trips laid upon him by slave-moralist rabbis, priests and political correctors, or their appeals to holy books, the "good of society" or "the children". The Dark Lord seeks to develop, from hard experience and deep reflection, a philosophy that can withstand any attack and become a mighty weapon of conquest in its own right, while staying mindful of the limitations of philosophy and the importance of worldly action. This book is written to give the aspiring Dark Lord the tools to do just that.

GENERAL CONSIDERATIONS

The Power of Philosophy

Philosophy is the study of the most fundamental concepts that order the world in every domain: metaphysics, mind, morality, politics, religion, science, ethics, law, war, etc. A philosopher seeks to identify and analyze the foundational ideas that govern the various domains of human thought and experience. As such, philosophy is both the most "useless" and impractical of activities, and potentially the most powerful.

To the extent that individual lives, groups, societies, nations and civilizations are founded on ideas, they are vulnerable to philosophy. Philosophers can unravel the fabric of a whole civilization with a single powerful idea—which is why, going back to the earliest philosophers such as Socrates, they have been viewed with suspicion and proscribed. Plato, the founding father of Western philosophy, held that philosophers had a duty to propagate "noble lies" that would placate the common people and uphold the state, rather than rile up citizens' minds with subversive ideas. Qin Shi Huang, the great conqueror and first emperor of unified China, is said to have buried numerous philosophers alive and burned their books for advocating ideas that were incompatible with his regime. Western civilization has been convulsed numerous times by philosophers: the moral and metaphysical innovations of

Jesus, Paul and other Christians overthrew the classical Greco-Roman regime; the theological challenges of Martin Luther shattered the Catholic monopoly on truth and plunged Christendom into a brutal thirty year war; the Enlightenment philosophers undermined the authority of the monarchical and theocratic orders and upended their societies; the communist philosophy of Marx, Engels and Lenin brought an "iron curtain" across Europe and inspired revolutions across the globe; postmodernists deconstructed the foundations of Western civilization and opened a Pandora's box of cultural transformations. Even in today's "liberal" societies, where thought is cheap and ideas a dime a dozen, philosophy remains quite dangerous: individuals may be proscribed, vilified, sued or marginalized for asking uncomfortable questions or holding "politically incorrect" opinions that that threaten the authority of the ruling regime.

There are many ways to seek and acquire power—military conquest, political machination, cultural creation, personal manipulation, etc.—but no endeavor is more ambitious or more potentially world-conquering than the method of philosophical inquiry which is the focus of this book.

The Limits of Philosophy

From the outset, we also recognize the limitations of philosophy that arise from the definition given above: that it is the study of *concepts,* which are ideas or thoughtforms originating in the neo-cortex of the brain. Philosophy is an exercise in cerebral thought, abstraction and language; it operates in the newest layer of the brain, where concepts are formed, and has no way of accessing or understanding the unconscious, ineffable layers of the mind where most mentation actually occurs. This problem has been recognized by Western philosophers since at least Nietzsche, informed by the psychological findings of Freud, explored in the work of Wittgenstein and Heidegger, experienced by modern "psychonauts" and quantified by neuroscientists. In the East, the limits of philosophy have been recognized for thousands of years, going back to the Prajnaparamita and Shunyata schools of Hinduism and Buddhism, and Taoism since its inception. Try as it might, philosophy, defined as a product of the rational, conceptualizing layer of mind, cannot be conducted in isolation from the deeper layers of mental activity, nor from any "mystical" influences that may affect it.

As Dark Lords, we are philosophers, but we are also mystics and Black Magicians who believe in the unlimited power of the mind. We therefore advocate a broadening of philosophical inquiry to include any activity that seeks to "know thyself" or "know the world" as part of a total science of mind power. In this book we will discuss philosophical concepts, but we will do so ever mindful of the unconscious, "Dark Side" realms of mind that fall outside of conventional Western philosophy and could be categorized as mysticism. The great failing of orthodox philosophy in our view has been its narrow focus on rational concepts and its dismissal of anything mystical or intuitive as having no truth-perceiving power. We find the reality to be quite the opposite: it is beyond the limits of conventional philosophy that one is likely to discover the profoundest truths.

First Principles

Power and Perception

The first principle of our philosophy is the recognition of the existence of an "I": of the individual consciousness that perceives and acts within the world in a way that separates it from everything else that exists. For each "I" perceives the world differently from every other being, if for no other reason than that our perceptive apparatus is housed in separate bodies. Each "I" also acts within the world differently, expressing its will in a distinct way as it proceeds on its unique path through life. This sense of individual perception and agency gives each of us our sense of being.

René Descartes, who has been called "the father of modern Western philosophy", formulated his first principle as: *ego cogito, ergo sum* ("I think, therefore I am"). But this maxim is insufficient, in our view. If one could only think, perhaps as some sort of disembodied intelligence or "brain in a vat", how would one even be conscious of one's own existence? Without sensory awareness to situate oneself in a world of external objects, and without an embodiment in that world that responds to one's thoughts, in what sense does one exist as a distinct entity in that world? Where does such an abstract intelligence exist, and what does it do?

The recognition of the primacy of one's individual *will* and *perception* is for us the beginning of being; it is the "ground of being" upon which all philosophy must be built. We could say that this sense of "I-ness" is the "spark of Godhood" that exists within all conscious beings, and which distinguishes them from unconscious matter. We use two words to capture the essence of this sense of independent being and agency: *power* and *perception*.

I-Theism

From these two first principles, we can proceed to develop our philosophy and ideology. As we do so, we will stay mindful of these primal facts, avoiding any currents of thought that would cloud our perceptions, weaken our wills or dissolve our sense of individual being. Here our elevation of the individual "I" to the highest philosophical position is at odds with most religious and mystical traditions, which advocate dissolving the self into a larger universal entity, such as "God", "the Void" or "Brahman". It also conflicts with many political ideologies, which advocate for identifying with a social collective, such as a nation, religious community, tribe, or humanity as a whole, above one's own independent will. But for our kind, there is no virtue in humbling oneself or dissolving one's ego in such a larger thoughtform. We regard it, in fact, as the greatest "sin" and "evil". For to seek the dissolution of the self is to deny our fundamental gift as individual beings; it amounts to philosophical suicide.

As Dark Lords, we advocate for the opposite extreme: rather than seeking to absorb the self in a larger macrocosm, we seek to absorb the macrocosm into the self. We seek to make everything subject to our own perception and volition; to become all-knowing and all-powerful; to become as gods. We call this philosophy *I-theism (nâm-zimodûn)*. As I-theists, we violently reject all philosophies and ideologies that preach ego-dissolution as slave moralistic, suicidal and unfit for our kind.

This does not imply that we are concerned with "liberating" or "empowering" the masses of humanity from their submission to various macrocosmic entities, whether they be gods, governments or philosophical thoughtforms. It is perfectly acceptable for a self-liberated Dark Lord to propagate an ideology of ego-submission for others, if it serves his own path of unlimited power. In fact, inspiring others to submit to your thoughtforms is one of the most potent techniques of ego-enhancement, and is to be encouraged and developed on the path to Dark Lordship. All the great Dark Lords of myth and history have used this methodology at some point; the conquerors, prophets and artists who propagated new religions, visions and regimes, were only successful because they were able to convince others that submission to their ideas was better than the alternatives. The masses of humanity, lacking the self-realization, imagination and inner power of Dark Lords, will forever look to our kind for inspiration, guidance and a source of authority to which to submit. Our challenge is to become beings to whom others willingly and enthusiastically do so.

The Source

Having said that the self is the supreme source of value for a Dark Lord, which is never to submit to any external entity, we make one crucial caveat. There may exist a thoughtform outside the Dark Lord to whom even he submits, though he submits to no other being in existence. This is the thoughtform we call *the Source (Tozg)*. Down through history, we find that the great prophets, kings and conquerors had such a Source to guide them. Alexander called himself the "son of Zeus"—sky-god and king of the Olympians; Roman emperors followed the prophecy of the same god, Jupiter, who granted them "empire without end"; Muhammad received commands directly from the one god Allah to make the world submit to his religion; the early Mongol Khans obeyed the sky-god Tengri, "by whom we live and by whom we die"; the mighty Popes of medieval Europe answered only to God in heaven; the Caliphs of the Islamic empire submitted to no earthly authority but Allah's will; and so on. We thus consider it acceptable, if not desirable, for a Dark Lord take such a Source as his highest font of inspiration and authority, if it serves to elevate him to a more exalted and powerful state and status. We ourselves gravitate toward Sources such as the "Dark Force", "Satan" and the "Black Sun" more than the sky-gods of the deserts and steppes, but that is a matter for the inspiration and taste of each Dark Lord to decide.

Endarkenment

These first principles aren't mere academic concerns. Philosophical maxims form the foundation of entire civilizations, and if those maxims are found to be false or disagreeable, it calls into question the entire civilization built upon them. For example, Descartes is considered the founder of modern rationalist philosophy, which laid the foundation for the "Enlightenment" movement, inspired the architects of the American and French Revolutions, and led to the rise of the modern "liberal", rationalist civilization that has spread across the world. Yet, at its foundation we find a philosophical error: the notion that existence can be reduced to abstract thought; that individual reasoning, separate from will, perception and the shadow-mind, can arrive at all truths that matter. Rationalists further compound the error by asserting that these truths will be agreed upon by all reasonable people, thus forming the foundation of liberal society, where notions of "rights", "equality" and "liberty" flow from the supposedly universal power of reason in human affairs.

Such dubious propositions have been challenged by many subsequent philosophers—notably Germans such as Schopenhauer, Nietzsche and Heidegger, "postmodernists" such as Foucault and Derrida, thinkers from a wide variety of spiritual and religious traditions, as well as modern psychologists, social scientists and neuroscientists. The weight of evidence suggests to us that the rationalist philosophy of Descartes et al., is erroneous and delusional;

that human beings are governed by irrational impulses of every sort that stubbornly elude rational analysis or control. It remains for bold Dark Side philosophers to tap into these irrational impulses so as to overthrow the rationalists' "Enlightenment" regime and initiate an age of "Endarkenment" that more accurately reflects the deep truths and longings of the shadow-mind.

Dark Side Philosophy

The Dark Side

If the Source is the place from which all gods and first principles emanate, then the *Dark Side (Ârz Bortâg)* refers to those aspects of the Source that are "dark", destructive, irrational, evil or unknown. The Dark Side takes many forms in different peoples' imaginations—the ancient gods Set, Ahriman, Kali, Typhon, Tezcatlipoca or Hecate, the Christian Devil, or more abstract conceptions such as the Black Sun. But the Dark Side itself is a Source beyond all forms, with its own ineffable nature and will.

We say that the Dark Side is the Source of the *Dark Force (Bor-Zy)*, which is the metaphysical energy that manifests the "will" of the Dark Side in individual beings and in the world at large. The Dark Force produces a myriad of dark "currents", which manifest as various cults, religions and philosophies that disrupt, awe and terrify the world.

One of the earliest references to the Dark Side in the history of ideas came from the Persian prophet Zoroaster, who spoke of *angra mainyu* ("destructive spirit") and *aka mainyu* ("evil spirit")—two terms that both capture the essence of the Dark Side. Zoroaster's philosophy was one of the first to divide the world into two opposing metaphysical poles, creating a primal "good and evil", "God and the Devil" polarity that greatly influenced Jewish, Christian and Muslim thought and continues to influence minds down to the present day. The metaphysics of the Star Wars universe is very much a product of Zoroaster's thought from more than three thousand years ago.

How does one come to know the Dark Side? It shows its face during those moments of wild terror that civilized man works so hard to eliminate from his experience, yet which still break through the facade of peace and order from time to time—during wars, riots, criminal acts, terrorist attacks, natural disasters, wild animal encounters, and so on. The Dark Side can be seen by simply observing any patch of nature, as stronger creatures devour weaker creatures, every being dies and all things decay and turn to dust. When the vicious visage of a wild dog is in your face, its hot breath and saliva touching your skin, its claws and fangs threatening to shred your flesh, you have felt the touch of the Dark Side. No amount of reasoned argument or moral appeal can stop such a beast, any more than it can stop the Dark Side. The Dark Side is the "wild dog of thought", which is immune to all rational philosophy and moralism.

Nevertheless, we can formulate some general tenets of *Dark Side philosophy (Bortâgodûn)*, which we summarize in the box below:

Dark Side Philosophy:

- Knowledge is acquired with both the conscious and unconscious, rational and irrational minds.
- There is no divine, benevolent or rational order to the world that determines absolute truth.

- Man is an irrational being, and he should cultivate irrationality in the pursuit of inspiration and power rather than deny it.
- There is no single correct answer to any question.
- More knowledge may be harmful; the pursuit of truth is neither inherently good nor bad.
- Truth is dependent on culture, power relations, individual experiences and perceptions.
- Death, predation and destruction are primal facts of life that trump other values.

Dark Side Schools of Thought

Dark Side philosophy is a general term for schools of thought that are strongly aware of, emanate from or give their allegiance to the Dark Side. Sithism *(Zithodûn)*, the primary subject of this book, is one particular school of Dark Side philosophy—the one subscribed to by members of the Sith Order. Sithism should not be confused with Dark Side philosophy as a whole, which encompasses many other schools of thought, including *Diabolism (Dârkorodûn), Black Ninjutsu (Bor-Rûdâr), Dark Mentalism (Bor-Hûzodûn), Black Sunnism (Borzûmodûn)* and *Chaoism (Klânodûn)*. Detailed discussions of such Dark Side philosophies may be found in other books by the Dark Lords, as already published or to be published in the future.

Light Side Philosophy

To understand any particular thing, it is necessary and useful to study that thing's opposite. Moreover, one should know one's enemy if one wishes to defeat him. Therefore, let us now discuss Light Side philosophy *(Mâltâgodûn)* in order to know the weaknesses of the opposing creed and gain a better understanding of our own path.

Light Side philosophy is concerned with studying concepts like "reality", "truth", "the good" and "justice" in the abstract, using reason as its primary tool. Leading exemplars of this philosophical orientation include Socrates, Aristotle, Aquinas, Descartes, Spinoza, Locke, Kant and Hegel. Western civilization has been dominated by Light Side philosophers since the time of Socrates. In the East, philosophy was traditionally more mystically inclined and not strictly Light Side—Confucius being a major exception.

Here are some of the major tenets we associate with Light Side philosophy:

Light Side Philosophy:

- Knowledge is acquired with the conscious, rational mind.
- There is a divine, benevolent or rational order to the world that provides an absolute standard of truth.
- Man is a rational being, and he should strive to become more rational in the pursuit of truth and the good.
- There is one correct, rational answer to every question.
- More knowledge is always to the good; the pursuit of truth is inherently good.

- There is an objective "truth" which is independent of social context and individual interpretation.
- Life, beneficence and creation are primal values that trump other values.

Light Side vs. Dark Side Philosophy

To sum it up simply, Light Side philosophy seeks to know the world with the conscious, rational mind, whereas Dark Side philosophy seeks to know the world with both the conscious and unconscious, rational and irrational minds. Dark Side philosophy consults the will as well as the intellect; the Dark Side philosopher does not merely ask what something *is* abstractly; he asks what should be *done* about it. In Dark Side philosophy, one must take into account psychology, power relations and culture in evaluating any philosophical proposition.

To illustrate these differences, consider the following example. Two prominent philosophers from opposing Light and Dark Side schools have agreed to hold a public debate on the main tenets of their schools of thought. The Light Side philosopher prepares for the event by reviewing the best arguments for his school's tenets, noting the chains of logic that support each one and appealing to the reason of the listener. He assumes that his arguments will be heard by others in good faith, who by their own reason will be persuaded of their truth. He doesn't spend any time thinking about his physical security for the debate.

The Dark Side philosopher, being a craftier sort of fellow, prepares for the debate in a rather different manner. He reviews the tenets of his school but doesn't spend any time thinking about their rational justifications. In fact he knows that these tenets are really *assertions*, and isn't interested in persuading others of their truth by reason alone. Instead, the Darksider meets with other members of his school, and they make plans for the day of the debate, which they keep to themselves.

The day of the debate arrives, and the two philosophers meet at the designated hall as scheduled. However, just as they are about to begin, a group of black-clad men rush the stage and seize the Light Side philosopher. The men hand the Lightsider a piece of paper and order him to read it. The Light Side philosopher, who is used to debating in safe environments against non-violent adversaries, is terrified and does as he as told. He reads the statement, which in effect concedes the debate to the Darksider and admits that the tenets of Dark Side philosophy are superior to his own. He states further that he is retiring from philosophy and will no longer promote Light Side philosophy publicly, then he is frog-marched off the stage by the Darksider's accomplices, to howls of protest from his supporters in the audience. The Darksider then briefly addresses the audience, surrounded by his men, triumphantly declaring another victory for their philosophy. Thus the debate is concluded.

The above scenario illustrates several weaknesses of Light Side philosophy. The Lightsider assumes that his opponent will play by Light Side rules; i.e., that the debate will be a rational discussion of abstractions—a purely mental exercise divorced from any acts of will or cultural assertions by the other side. Because Light Side philosophers imagine that truth is only arrived at via conscious, rational dialectics, they overlook the possibility that the other side will use "irrational" or "will to power" tactics, and consider them invalid means of asserting philosophical truth. To the Lightsider, the Darksiders have violated the spirit of philosophy, engaged in an "evil" act or "cheated". To the Darksiders, such acts are fair game because philosophy does not exist in some realm of pure ideals, divorced from the cultural and power imperatives of its society. Thus the Darksiders have given the Lightsiders an object lesson in the truth of their philosophy. The Lightsiders may insist that the other side has not won anything, but in the real world of conflicting, subjective truths, where there is no absolute standard of truth, what else can decide any debate but "might is right"? By appealing to reason or justice in his protest, the Lightsider is committing a fallacy of believing in an absolute standard, which the Darksiders, who also argue with their "shadow-minds" (and fists), are free to reject.

PHILOSOPHY OF POWER, EVIL AND WAR

POWER

The Way of Power

The philosophy of Sithism can be summarized as the *Way of Power*, or *Râkodûn*. The primary questions of Sithism are things like: What is the nature of power? What is the source of power? Who has power? How is power acquired? How is power increased? Sith philosophy is not a search for "truth" in some abstract sense, but the search for answers to such questions. Sithism takes as its first principle the existence and primacy of power; it does not critique or "deconstruct" power, except in so far as that may lead to still greater power. Sith philosophers do not criticize the powerful for their excesses of power, or make moral appeals in an attempt to shame them, as is so often done in modern "liberal", "democratic", "slave moralist" societies. Rather, they criticize them for their lack of power, weakness of will and poverty of ambition. Everything in a society governed by Sithism is subordinated to the all-consuming quest for power. Science seeks to know how nature works so that it may increase human power over it; technology seeks to extend the human will via machines and thus increase human power; culture seeks to increase the power of those who produce it and the society that supports it; religion does the same; intellectuals analyze problems in terms of their relationship to power, and what is best for power. Power, to a Sith philosopher, functions much as "Truth", "God" or "the Good" does to a Light Side thinker: it is the highest source of our values, authority and purpose.

Understand that when we speak of Sithism as a philosophy of power, we are speaking of power in all its forms. We do not refer only to the power to rule over others, to dominate their wills and defeat them militarily or politically. Power includes all those things that make a person compelling: competence, creativity, charisma, mystique, knowledge, wisdom, vitality, etc. Power also includes the use of myth, art and literature, spiritual leadership, seduction, esoteric practice and tradition. There is no aspect of life that does not act in the service of power.

What separates a Sith from any other powerful person? Is the Pope Sith? The difference lies in how one uses one's power. If power is used in the service of a Light Side ideal then it is not Sith. A president, spiritual leader or artist promoting peace, equality or obedience to a Light Side god as their highest values is not Sith. A leader who deprecates power itself is not Sith. In truth, there are precious few powerful people in this age who are consciously promoting Dark Side values, and even fewer who make themselves known as such.

The Four Dimensions of Power
Power refers to the ability to manifest one's will in any sphere of activity. As we see it, there are four primary dimensions of power, as follows.

Inner Power: the ability to compel your own mind and body to obey your will (willpower), to be self-reliant, unconquerable and have an inner sense of purpose (Will).

Personal Power: The ability to compel other beings to act in desired ways, alter their personalities or beliefs, seduce them, etc.

Political Power: The ability to compel groups of people to follow your will, manipulate crowds and steer the destinies of nations.

Metaphysical Power: The ability to operate on the planes of mind, myth and magick to alter the fabric of subjective or objective reality. Includes the use of rituals, language, symbols and arts to invoke Force power from a Source, such as God, the Devil or the Black Sun.

These four types of power are linked and ordered; one drives another in a hierarchy of manifestation. The proper order of power manifestation in our view is this:

> metaphysical power → inner power → personal power → political power

This chain of power manifestation entails four steps:

> Identify a Source and invoke Force power from it →
>
> Fuel your will and sense of purpose with that Force →
>
> Infect others with your enthusiasm for your Source or dominate them with your strong, purposeful will →
>
> Infect or dominate large groups of people directly, or manipulate them via leaders you control

There is an outstanding passage in the novel ***Darth Plagueis*** that nicely describes this process of power flow. Here Darth Sidious (Palpatine) is reflecting on his life and the teachings of his master, Darth Tenebrous:

> But Palpatine was grateful, for the Force had slowly

groomed him into a being of dark power and granted him a secret identity, as well. The life he had been leading—as the noble head of House Palpatine, legislator, and most recently ambassador-at-large—was nothing more than the trappings of an alter ego; his wealth, a subterfuge; his handsome face, a mask. In the realm of the Force his thoughts ordered reality, and his dreams prepared the galaxy for monumental change. He was a manifestation of dark purpose, helping to advance the Sith Grand Plan and gradually gaining power over himself so that he might one day—in the words of his Master—be able to gain control over another, then a group of others, then an order, a world, a species, the Republic itself.

There you have it, directly from the mind of the great Sith Lord of legend. Just four steps to unlimited power and Galactic Empire—what are you waiting for?

Will Power

Sithism, as a philosophy that posits the primacy of inner power, works primarily upon the will. Its main aim is to inflame, empower and direct the will of the Acolyte, not to tickle his cerebrum with abstractions or subjugate his mind to rational thoughts in the manner of Western philosophy. Some would say this not philosophy, but we don't see it that way. A mind is more than intellect or reason; it contains a deep reservoir of unconscious and irrational impulses that no complete philosophy of life can ignore. Where the rationalist philosopher argues in chains of logic and appeals to reason, the irrationalist philosopher makes assertions of will and appeals to the imagination. This is still philosophy, it simply expands our notion of philosophy to include the "shadow-mind" or subconscious, reptilian brain where the will operates. Rationalist philosophy is concerned with the "tip of the iceberg" of the mind that is easily accessible; Sith philosophy is interested in the whole iceberg —particularly the submerged 90% which can only be seen by going into the murky depths, which may not look important on the surface, but gives the iceberg its mass, volume, stability, and ship-sinking power.

Evil

> "Evil? What is that? ...You said you were death itself. Are you evil, then, or are you simply stronger and more awake than others? Who gives more shape to sentient history: the good, who adhere to the tried and true, or those who seek to rouse beings from their stupor and lead them to glory? A storm you are, but a much needed one, to wash away the old and complacent and prune the galaxy of deadweight." —Darth Plagueis to Apprentice Palpatine

Darth Sidious once told Annakin Skywalker that "good is a point of view"; and so is evil. Here is our point of view on some aspects of existence that many call "evil".

Evilution

The nature of life in this world reveals itself in the forms of the beasts who inhabit it. We observe the fangs, claws, horns and hides, the stealth, speed, strength, cunning and ferocity of nature's apex species, and it tells us that they are warriors—the descendants of lines of winners of the wars for life that have raged across this planet for all the bloody eons since life began.

But what of man? How did such a frail, fang-less, claw-less, thin-skinned, clumsy monkey ever rise to a position of global dominance? Surely life does not evolve toward redder fangs and sharper claws, or man would never have survived his first encounters with the tiger-hunted jungle floor. The answer, of course, is that man's fangs and claws exist between his ears; he has developed his brain into a weapon of war without parallel in this planet's history. Man may lack natural weaponry, but he crafts it as naturally as a tiger stalks a gazelle. And what weapons he crafts! Arms lethal enough to kill any beast, hunt whole species to extinction, wage wars of extermination, annihilate civilizations and destroy entire planets in atomic hellfire. So powerful is his mental arsenal by now that no other beast can threaten him; man's only enemy on this planet is himself. We are a "breakaway species"—the beneficiaries of an evolutionary leap that has allowed us to terrorize all other species and reshape the planetary environment to our advantage.

Charles Darwin famously formulated the theory of *evolution*: survival of the most well-adapted species in the struggle for life. We posit the theory of *evilution*: survival of the most lethal, the most devious, the most evil species in said struggle. We are the proof that life evolves not toward redder claws and thicker hides, but more powerful and evil minds. For what species can compare to humans for capacity for cruelty? What species has unleashed more death, destruction and horror upon this planet than us? Humanity has no doubt made a quantum leap and set a new high-water mark in the process of evilution, but we are not the end state of evil. In the future, we can expect something even more evil to arise, quite likely of man's own making: a demonic super-race or Satanic machine superintelligence that terrorizes homo sapiens as we have terrorized the other beasts, and which ultimately enslaves, eats or exterminates us as we have done to them. And that is as it must be, in this War Universe ruled by evilution.

Predation

The ecosystems of life on this planet consist of predators

and prey, coexisting in a finely tuned balance that prevents overpopulation and degeneration and provides a catalyst for evolution. Predation is necessary for the vitality of living systems for several reasons: first, because all life must feed on other life to survive; second, because predators act as "eco-police" that prevent other species from overrunning their environment, consuming its resources and causing the ecosystem to collapse; third, because predators cull the weakest members of prey species and thus maintain the latter's genetic fitness; fourth, because predation rewards intelligence and innovation; predators must outsmart their prey to survive, which creates an evolutionary incentive for them to become ever smarter and more inventive—a process which has produced the most clever of all predatory species to date, homo sapiens.

The vital necessity of predation is not abstract philosophy; it has been observed many times in nature. For example, when early conservationists attempted to make game reserves and national parks safe for the tourists and animals by killing off the wolves and other apex predators, the result was disaster. Over time, the health of the preserve's animals deteriorated; prey species reproduced out of control, overgrazed the forests, their sickly members survived and the health of the species declined. By disrupting the natural balance of predators and prey, the human meddlers were damaging the entire ecosystem and causing long-term harm to the species they were trying to protect. So they were forced to reintroduce wolves into the parks, which led to a restoration of the balance and the revitalization of the ecosystem in short order. This is a powerful lesson for those humans who imagine that nature has any respect for their notions of morality, or that predation can be eliminated without dire consequences. Nature, being "red in tooth and claw", has its own morality, which is totally at odds with

Judeo-Christian moralism—which, let's recall, originated in deserts that were once green and full of life.

These principles can be extended to the realms of philosophy, morality and politics as well. Just as trying to eradicate predators leads to ecological imbalance and sickness, trying to eradicate various "evils" that have vital functions in human societies will lead to societal stagnation, dysfunction and demoralization. Why do "wars on crime" never win? Because criminals provide products and services the population wants, whether that be drugs, prostitution, gambling, or what have you. Thieves and murderers make billions of dollars for the security industry; the threat of war and terrorism makes trillions for the military-industrial complex; the specter of sin and evil keeps the churches coffers full; and so on. If such predatory forces were suddenly eliminated, the economies of the civilized world would immediately collapse.

Predators also give shepherds and ranchers a justification for their existence. In a dangerous world full of wolves, the sheep must be protected by fences, sheepdogs and shepherds with guns. This is a good metaphor for the institutions of civilization, such as governments, laws, police, military and churches. It is the threats of the predators—criminals, terrorists, evil-doers, enemy nations—that provide the institutions with their strongest justification for existence and their source of authority. "We are protecting you from the wolves", say the shepherds of civilization; "without us, you would be at their mercy, and they have none". Thus we have a situation where the shepherds have a parasitic relationship to the predators; they need predators to exist and be strong, for if the predators disappeared, the shepherds would no longer be needed. This phenomenon is common in every civilization, where the forces of law, order and security regularly puff up the threats of predators and promise to wage "wars on crime/terror/evil" in order to increase their own power.

On an ideological level, predation is necessary to prevent intellectual stagnation, spiritual degeneration and the proliferation of pathological ideas. We saw a good example of this with the Communist regimes of the 20th century, as they attempted to eliminate the predators known as "capitalists" and "aristocrats" and stamp out all politically incorrect thought. This resulted not in the end of predation and the onset of cooperative socialist utopias, but the advent of a new predatory class in the form of the Communist party elites, who often became more vicious predators that the ones they replaced. But since they had gained their positions more by ideological allegiance than long experience and proven skill at predation, they were unable to fill the shoes of the previous predatory classes. These Communists, like the early conservationists, were ideologically blind to the fact that human and animal ecosystems reward and require predation. This disconnect between ideology and reality proved disastrous. Economies stagnated, innovation lagged, and the Communist nations were unable to compete with the highly innovative, predatory economies of the capitalist West. Using our national park metaphor, the Communists attempted to eliminate the successful predators, replace them with park managers, and turn their societies into human game preserves. Not surprisingly, their attempts to engineer their societies to conform to Light Side ideological notions that failed to respect the role of predation failed miserably. This led eventually to the "reintroduction of the wolves", in the form of the return of capitalists and gangsters to ex-Communist nations like China and Russia. This has revitalized their stagnant economies, brought a surge of innovation and confidence, and made them feared animals in the jungle of nations once more.

On a personal note, the Dark Lords, having experienced both ends of the predator-prey, capitalist-communist spectrum themselves, can say without a doubt that we prefer the predatory end. We would never be what we are today if we had not had the experience of making significant quantities of money in rather gangster-like fashion. The experiences of power, innovation, freedom, sovereignty and vitality that we have had as predatory capitalists surely surpass anything available to us as victimized communists. You want to know the power of the Dark Side? Try surviving as a predatory capitalist in a dog-eat-dog society, and you will get a taste of it quick, fast and in a hurry!

To conclude, Sith philosophers should function in the realm of ideas and spirit like the wolf or the lion in the animal kingdom: as apex predators, who prey upon weak ideas, force them to fight, flee or die, and in the process eliminate those which are unfit to survive from the memetic ecosystem. In this way, we drive the ideological evolution of the world, becoming effectively vitalizing agents of the evolutionary and evilutionary process.

A Sinister Path

There are those who would like a sugar-coated Sithism that is a path of rugged individualism, "self-improvement", social Darwinism, martial arts and atheism. In their view, the Sith should be philosophically akin to Ayn Rand-reading "Objectivists", 19th century British imperialists, modern American capitalists or LaVeyan "Satanists". I.e., the Sith should be little more than materialistic, mundane seekers after power, who may be highly successful within the modern capitalist milieu but don't threaten it philosophically in any significant way.

We strongly disagree with this conception of Sithism. We believe that real Sith must possess a special inner darkness and metaphysical perception; an aura of power, evil and menace; a timeless, numinous quality that David Myatt, the evil genius behind the *Order of Nine Angles,* calls the *sinister.* This is the quality you sense in Darth Maul in *The Phantom Menace:* a dangerous, demonic presence, in a being who is not like other men—a dark superman capable of transgressing and destroying everything you hold dear. A Sith is a truly sinister being, whom mundanes will know immediately is not their kind; he is an alien from another age and world, with radically different ideas about what is good and possible. We call this special quality of numinous menace *kyâzik* in our Black Tongue. We say that Sithism is a *kyâzik-vodûn*—a sinister path to greatness, whose aim is to cultivate *kyâzik-hûz—sinister mind—*in its disciples.

WAR

If there is one fact that affirms Sith philosophy, it is the eternal existence and central importance of war in human affairs. War evinces at least six of Sithism's philosophical Pillars (see "The Nine Pillars of Sithism"):

The Primacy of Power: war drives men to acquire power like nothing else, for they know that lack of power means defeat on the battlefield, and the potential loss of everything they value—sovereignty, nation, culture and life.

The Tao of Darwin: war is the ultimate "survival of the fittest" contest that drives the evolution of technology, culture and even genetics—it is an instrument of Darwinism on the scale of nations and civilizations.

The Power of the Dark Side: war brings into the open the dark aspects of human minds, societies and nature that times of peace keep hidden, and rewards those who face and harness their dark sides most effectively.

The Force: war arouses powerful passions in the combatants —i.e. it generates Force energy—and it punishes the apathetic and the Forceless with defeat. War asks the ultimate questions of men: what do you believe in and what will you fight for?

The Superman: war awakens dormant powers within individual beings, driving them to great acts of will, genius, heroism and courage. By breaking the conditions of peaceful, comfortable existence, war forces men to become greater by life-and-death tests and trials.

Galactic Empire: war makes possible the creation of empires, and drives the upward evolution of power structures from tribe to city-state to nation to continental empire, leading perhaps to planetary empires and the conquest of the stars.

For all these reasons, we conclude that war is essential to human evolution, vitality and greatness, and cannot be eradicated without eradicating the very spirit which has driven all life upward from slime to man to superman. To condemn and seek the elimination of all war is therefore to commit a profound philosophical error, to believe in childish delusions and to be antithetical to the spirit of life itself. For we live indeed in a war universe, or *shâz-vrâthûl*, and cannot avoid war so long as we do. We must instead prepare for war, study war strategy and tactics, and engage in war with supreme will and excellence when necessary in order to achieve victory.

But it should also be understood that when we speak of war we do not mean impersonal, mechanized slaughter for meaningless abstractions or other people's benefit, as much of modern warfare has become. War for our kind is *holy war (zâkshâz)*: struggle for our own Source; fighting for the power of our Force Order; inner struggle against personal weakness and the forces of Light Side degeneration; conflict in the pursuit of individual and collective greatness. We do not wage meaningless wars or other men's wars (though we are not adverse to profiting from them). We understand that war has both inner and outer dimensions: a spiritual and personal purpose, a larger macrocosmic goal and an ultimate cosmic function. This multi-dimensional understanding of the value and significance of war is what we call *shâzodûn (warriorism)*, and the mindset it engenders is *shâzor-hûzûk*–warrior mentality.

The Eternal Warrior

The awakening to the nature of this War Universe should not come merely as a rational realization to the Sith Acolyte, but as a gnosis or an "ontological shock". He must become aware and ever-mindful of the fact that he lives in a War Universe and he has no choice but to fight. This realization is similar to the one described by Carlos Castaneda when his master, Don Juan, tells him:

> "When a man embarks on the paths of sorcery he becomes aware, in a gradual manner, that ordinary life has been forever left behind; that knowledge is indeed a frightening affair; that the means of the ordinary world are no longer a buffer for him; and that he must adopt a new way of life if he is going to survive. The first thing he ought to do, at that point, is to want to become a warrior. The frightening nature of knowledge leaves one no alternative but to become a warrior."

The Sith Acolyte who embarks on the path to Dark Lordship has no choice but to become a warrior. The disturbing nature of Dark Side knowledge requires him to adopt a new mentality and way of life. He must leave ordinary life behind forever and walk a path for the ages. In this way, he becomes more than a mundane man; he becomes a living embodiment of a thoughtform we call the *Eternal Warrior (Vrâzashik Shâzor)*.

The Eternal Warrior dwells outside of time; he travels through many bodies and lives through many lifetimes, but he is an undying thoughtform existing beyond this mortal plane. The Eternal Warrior knows that ages of peace are passing, tenuous and temporary; he has seen them come and go down through the centuries, and watched them fall always to new ages of war. In times of peace and comfort, the values of the Eternal Warrior may seem harsh, barbaric and unnecessary to those who have known nothing else. But the Eternal Warrior knows that such times are transient and its values fleeting. When times of strife return, it is to his kind that people look for strength, guidance and inspiration.

War Quotes

War philosophy has been reflected upon by great thinkers down through the ages; below are some of our favorite quotes on the subject.

> "War is the father and king of all: some he has made gods, and some men; some slaves and some free." – Heraclitus
>
> "There is no avoiding war; it can only be postponed to the advantage of others." –Niccolò Machiavelli
>
> "You say it is the good cause that justifies even war? I

say to you: it is the good war which justifies every cause."

"One has renounced the great life when one renounces war."

"I welcome all signs that a more virile, warlike age is about to begin, which will restore honor to courage above all. For this age shall prepare the way for one yet higher, and it shall gather the strength that this higher age will require one day—the age that will carry heroism into the search for knowledge and that will wage wars for the sake of ideas and their consequences."

"Religious War has signified the greatest advance of the masses so far, for it proves that the masses have begun to treat concepts with respect."

"The beginnings of everything great on earth [are] soaked in blood thoroughly and for a long time."

—Friedrich Nietzsche

"The great questions of the day will not be settled by means of speeches and majority decisions but by iron and blood." —Otto von Bismarck

"War is to man what maternity is to a woman. From a philosophical and doctrinal viewpoint, I do not believe in perpetual peace." —Benito Mussolini

"War, it is said, offers man the opportunity to awaken the hero who sleeps within him. War breaks the routine of comfortable life; by means of its severe ordeals, it offers a transfiguring knowledge of life, life according to death. The moment the individual succeeds in living as a hero, even if it is the final moment of his earthly life, weighs infinitely more on the scale of values than a protracted existence spent consuming monotonously among the trivialities of cities. From a spiritual point of view, these possibilities make up for the negative and destructive tendencies of war, which are one-sidedly and tendentiously highlighted by pacifist materialism. War makes one realise the relativity of human life and therefore also the law of a 'more-than-life', and thus war has always an anti-materialist value, a spiritual value." —Julius Evola

"But we have never stopped it [war] and never shall, because war is not the law of one age or civilization, but of eternal nature itself, out of which every civilization proceeds, and into which it must sink again if it is not hard enough to withstand its iron ordeal." —Ernst Jünger

METAPHYSICS

BUILDING BLOCKS OF REALITY

Metaphysics is the study of what existence or reality consists of at its most fundamental level. Is the world composed only of matter and energy? Are there non-material forces that affect the material world? Do gods exist? What is being? What is mind? What is time? These are examples of the kinds of questions metaphysics seeks to answer. In this chapter we survey some of the metaphysical ideas that are most relevant to Sith philosophy, and some of our own ideas about them.

Panpsychism

In our black magickal worldview, we recognize and glorify the unlimited power of the mind to perceive, order and manipulate reality. We do not believe that the mind is merely a byproduct of the biochemical processes of the brain, nor is it limited in time and space, nor must it obey the physical laws of matter and energy. The mind is the primal substance from which reality is constructed; it permeates space and time, and what we think of as our individual minds are really nodes or receivers of a super-consciousness that transcends and lives on beyond them. Consciousness animates everything to some degree; even the simplest particle contains a rudimentary intelligence. The entire cosmos is intelligent, and by enhancing our connection to the universal mind, we may obtain unlimited awareness, insight and power.

These beliefs are consistent with the doctrine of *panpsychism*—the idea that mind is a fundamental and universal aspect of reality. Most human cultures throughout history have embraced some form of panpsychism, from archaic animistic and shamanism to paganism, pre-Socratic philosophy to Neoplatonism, Eastern philosophies such as Taoism, Hinduism and Buddhism, to more recent thinkers such as Gottfried Leibniz, Arthur Schopenhauer, William James, Carl Jung and Aldous Huxley. Panpsychism fell out of favor in the West over the past few centuries with the rise of scientific materialism and rationalism, which found no measurable evidence for a universal mind nor any logical necessity for its existence. However, at the fringes of science, in fields such as psychic research, and increasingly among reputable philosophers, panpsychism appears to be gaining favor as a means to explain various puzzles such as psychic phenomena and the "mind-body problem" of how minds emerge from matter. In a panpsychic universe, ESP phenomena are understood as powers of a non-local, universal mind that individual minds have access to. The mind-body problem doesn't exist, since all things consist fundamentally of mind—i.e. the world is *monistic* (consisting of one thing) rather than *dualistic* (consisting of two things —mind and matter).

In our magickal tongue, we call the doctrine of panpsychism *vrâhûzodûn ("all mind-ism")*. We do not attempt rationally prove this doctrine, but take the following statement of its basic principle as intuitively true:

> Consciousness is a fundamental building block of reality. Mind is embedded in the structure of the cosmos. The potential for consciousness exists in every atom and every cubic centimeter of the void. The perception and influence of consciousness

extends over the entire material universe.

This principle makes possible the magickal universe which all Sith believe in. Our existence as black magicians and Lords of the Force requires a panpsychic universe, so it is a self-serving philosophy. How could black magicians who seek to conquer the universe with super-powered minds believe anything else? Our philosophy must serve our wills...which brings us to our next metaphysical doctrine.

Panbolism

The second doctrine from which we construct our metaphysics is one that marks us fully as black magicians, who rank the will at least equal to the intellect as a metaphysical force. Here we introduce a term which to our knowledge has never been used before: *panbolism*. "Bol" comes from the ancient Greek word "boule", meaning "will" or "volition". In Borgâl, we call it *vrâzhinodûn ("all-will-ism")*.

The doctrine of panbolism is the following:

Volition is a fundamental building block of reality. Will is embedded in the structure of the cosmos. Everything that exists, from the simplest particles to the most complex structures of matter, from microbes to human beings, from simple ideas to the most complex thoughtforms, has an associated will that drives it toward some goal or purpose. Furthermore, these wills are connected: the potential influence of any source of volition extends over the entire material universe.

Panbolism identifies volition as a second universal force, in addition to consciousness or perception. It adds "I will, therefore I am" to "I think, therefore I am" as universal statements of being. In book two of this series, ***Masters of*** *the Will*, we spoke of *the Will* as the transpersonal, "cosmic will" that gives beings their deep, mythic sources of motivation. We say that this universal will emanates from *the Source*, via the mechanism of *the Force*. All of this is consistent with a panbolist understanding of reality.

Panbolism is an intuitive belief, but it is supported by empirical facts. We observe that all life-forms have wills which compel them to survive and propagate. The evolution (or evilution) of life can be thought of as an expression of the universal will. We observe volition even in "dead matter": we can think of gravity pulling objects toward an object as the "will" of the planet, star or black hole; flow of electricity is the "will" of electrons in a wire; cosmological expansion is the "will" of the universe as a whole. At the quantum level, particles whose behavior cannot be precisely predicted by any known method could be described as making choices—i.e. they have free will, and are exercising volition.

A Magickal Universe

Panpsychism and panbolism give us the metaphysical building blocks of a magickal universe. They imply that the entire cosmos is subject to the influence of our thoughts and will; that each of us is potentially a magician of unlimited power. This understanding has been called the "Law of Attraction" and "the power of positive thinking" by modern Lightsiders, but is an ancient principle known to all great magicians and men of power, whether of the Light Side or the Dark.

This magickal metaphysics threatens the power of many priesthoods, whether they posit a world proscribed by the laws of a moralistic god, or a universe made of dead matter which may only be known and mastered by the methods of materialist science. We reject both metaphysical positions as dead ends—as in effect magic circles drawn by opposing priesthoods to entrap and control humanity. In their place we posit a magickal universe *(chazik-vrâthûl)* of unlimited possibilities—but only for those bold souls able to liberate themselves from the mental prisons of the opposing orders, and take hold of the terrifying power that is our birthright in this magickal world.

It is worth noting that modern science itself supports the magickal universe theory. For unlike the mechanistic models of Newtonian physics, quantum physics suggests that no measurable events exist separate from the consciousness of the observers. If the physical universe is only that which we can measure, then quantum theory suggests that the physical universe is the creation of our minds.

Thoughtforms

The magickal universe brings another metaphysical possibility: that we not only have the potential to perceive and influence objects across the universe, but to *create* them. The mind can in effect materialize objects that exist not only in your own subjective perceptions, but in the perceptions of others. This is the phenomenon Tibetans call the *tulpa*; in English it is the *thoughtform;* in Borgâl, the *kurzât-chan*.

A thoughtform is an entity created by human belief: gods prayed to; demons invoked by rituals; superheroes celebrated in popular culture; governments authorized by constitutions; corporations created by laws; etc. A thoughtform is an object of collective belief that assumes its own independent existence, or a meme that takes on a life of its own. Whether a thoughtform is described as a collective hallucination, a social construct, the product of mass hypnosis, a magickal evocation, a meme, a demon or spirit, a divine manifestation, an unidentified flying object, or an expression of the "collective unconscious" doesn't change the nature of the phenomenon. Whatever is happening here is one of the most powerful phenomena in the human sphere, which we find at the foundations of religions, nations and social movements of all kinds. To name one notable example, the entire Abrahamic religious tradition began with a series of thoughtforms that appeared to the ancient Israelites en masse, and were interpreted as messages from God. Later, Jesus and Muhammad became new thoughtforms that inspired vast new branches to the Abrahamic tradition and dramatically altered the course of history. Whether one believes in such thoughtforms or dismisses them as collective illusions is beside the point, and potentially as foolish as dismissing belief in God as illusory while a mob of monotheists is converging on your home to burn you at the stake!

As black magicians, we consider thoughtforms real if they can wield such power over the human will and imagination. Our concern is not to prove or disprove them, but to harness them for our own purposes. Rather than attributing such phenomena to external agencies such as God or Satan, we take the view that they can be created by the fully developed minds of Dark Lords. Thus do we seek to "play God" by developing these powers ourselves. This is a view shared by modern chaos magicians, Tibetan lamas, Hindu yogis, Hermetic philosophers and ancient shamanic traditions since ancient times. The ability to harness the power of the gods via thoughtforms is one of the great "forbidden fruits", which the Abrahamic religions in particular have sought to proscribe and forbid, so that man remains subservient to their sky-god and priesthoods rather than seeking such power for himself. Thoughtforms are thus a vital weapon in the arsenals of anyone on a "Left Hand Path" of power, such as the Dark Lords of the Sith.

While this may all be very interesting as philosophy, it is even more interesting when one applies it by creating actual thoughtforms that appear as objective realities in other peoples' minds. Unfortunately, this is an advanced topic that is beyond the scope of this book. It may take months or years of learning various meditation, visualization, and manifestation techniques under the guidance of a Master to get results. More on the subject of thoughtforms will be made available to the dedicated Apprentice who shows an aptitude for such skills.

BLACK SUNNITE METAPHYSICS

Now we lay out more of the metaphysics that underlies Sithism and other black magickal projects being spearheaded by the Dark Lords. This material will be expanded on in *"Book of the Black Sun"*, to be published at a later date.

Two-Sun Philosophy

The Dark Lords hold to a worldview they call *Vorzûm-Zovrâd (Two-Sun Philosophy)*. According to this philosophy, there are two primary metaphysical "Suns"—the *Black Sun (Borzûm)* and the *White Sun (Mâlzûm)*—which influence the human Will and guide our destinies. The Black Sun is the source of *Bor-Zy*—the "dark Force" that compels men to conquer, fear, hate, destroy, die, follow dark gods and celebrate the darker aspects of existence. The White Sun is the source of *Mâl-Zy*—the "Light" spoken of in many religions, associated with love, life, healing, peace, benevolent gods and the "sunny side of life".

While the Dark Lords believe in the existence of both Suns, they consider the Black Sun to be dominant in this 'verse—as shown by the fact that the stars evolve into black holes, all life dies, everything crumbles into dust and the entire universe is going dark. Since Bor-Zy is stronger than Mâl-Zy in this life, they have chosen to cultivate it more than the weaker White Sun energy. This is what makes them *Dark Lords* and not *Light Lords!*

The Dark Lords also speak of two 'Temples' associated with the Two Suns: the *Black Sun Temple* and the *White Sun Temple*. These are not physical Temples, but abstract, metaphysical places—the *Black Lodge* and *White Lodge* spoken of in Theosophical and occult circles, where the followers of the Two Suns imaginally congregate.

Religions throughout history have recognized the reality of the Two-Sun duality: that there are two metaphysical poles which influence the human Will, and indeed all things. The Taoists called these poles *Yin* and the *Yang*; the Zoroastrians named them *Ahura Mazda,* god of light, and *Ahriman,* god of darkness; the Manicheans spoke of the world as a battleground of light and darkness; the Christians call them *God* and *the Devil*; Gnostics and Luciferians speak of the "light-bringer", enemy of the dark "demiurge" who rules this world; the fictional Jedi and Sith have their "light side" and "dark side" of the Force; and so on.

The Dark Lords also hold to an *Aeonic* worldview: that there are metaphysical ages, or *Aeons,* dominated by Black Sun consciousness, and others ruled by the White Sun. They believe the world is now entering a very dark *Black Sun Aeon (Borzûm-Olug),* but they also believe this process can be influenced by human Will. Thus, when Black Templars conduct rituals invoking the Black Sun and do other deeds, they are hastening the dawn of a Black Sun Aeon.

It should be noted that while the Dark Lords favor the Bor-Zy of the Black Sun, they do not deny the power of the Mâl-Zy of the White Sun. They simply see the White Sun as a weaker, fleeting emanation within the all-encompassing primordial Darkness. As Darth Imperius put it: "The Light that birthed this universe was a fleeting whim; the galaxies are growing dim; the Darkness will forever more ascend." The Dark Lords build Temples to the superior power of the Black Sun, and internalize its Darkness within themselves. This state is called *Endarkenment (Zhamboragûl)*.

Black Sun and White Sun Forces

In Black Sunnite metaphysics, the Two Suns are the primal duality, the "yin" and "yang" poles, whose interplay gives rise to the myriad of dualities that give existence its forms. The White Sun is the creative pole that said "Let there be Light" at the genesis of this universe; the Black Sun is destructive pole that draws the creations of Light back into the Void from whence they came. This duality of creative and destructive poles gives rise to a flow of force, just as the duality of the positive and negative terminals of a battery gives rise to a flow of electricity. This force flow manifests as flows of matter, energy and "dark energy" obeying physical laws in the realm of matter; it also manifests as ideas, thoughtforms and magickal currents obeying metaphysical laws in the realm of mind.

For example, in the realm of matter, the entire universe could be described as a flow of energy from the White Sun at the beginning of creation to the Black Sun at the end of time. The galaxies formed out of the primal White Sun, or "Big Bang", and are flying apart, diffusing and ultimately disintegrating into the Void of the primal Black Sun, driven by the force between the two metaphysical poles.

The Two Suns have different metaphysical natures, which are reflected in the effects of the forces that emanate from them. *Dark Force (Bor-Zy)* is associated with death, destruction, fear, harm, conflict and the unknown; *Light Force (Mâl-Zy)* is associated with life, creation, love, peace, healing and conscious knowledge. These two solar forces battle in endless cycles of creation and destruction in the realms of matter. In the realms of mind and myth, they play out individually and collectively as endless dramas of good versus evil, progress versus regress, hope versus despair, consciousness versus unconsciousness, and so on.

The Two Sides of the Force

We have spoken of the Two-Sun duality of the White Sun and the Black Sun, or the "Light Side" and "Dark Side" of the Force, but what do these terms actually mean? How do these two Force polarities manifest in our minds and in the world? The table below lists some conceptual dualities to illustrate the two Force polarities.

WHITE SUN	BLACK SUN
Conscious	Unconscious
Rational	Irrational
Known	Unknown
Creation	Destruction
Love	Hate
Shunning Fear	Embracing Fear
Peace	War
Life	Death
Blessing	Cursing

Healing	Harming
Progress	Entropy

Note that these are not moral categories. A person might be attracted to art that celebrates death, destruction or irrationality, without wanting to do "evil" in the conventional sense. A *Darksider (Bortâgor)* is simply one who recognizes that these darker phenomena are powerful aspects of existence, as fundamental as birth, creation or rationality. Furthermore, the Darksider gains Bor-Zy from these phenomena, developing a passion for death or finding inspiration in irrationality, so for him these dark aspects become "good". In the *Borzûmik ("Black Sunny")* worldview, "good" means "that which gives you Bor-Zy, makes you more powerful and passionate", and "bad" means "that which takes your Bor-Zy, weakens you and makes you apathetic". Our kind are those who find this kind of good in the Black Sun values, and are demoralized, depressed and sapped of Bor-Zy by the values of the White Sun. For example, a Black Sunnite would lose Bor-Zy at a "peace and love" New Age gathering or a Christian Church service—possibly even becoming physically ill. Conversely, she would be invigorated by the sight of soldiers marching off to war, a dog fight or a White Sunnite temple being demolished.

The Chaos-Form-Void Cycle

In Black Sunnite metaphysics we say that there are three states that characterize all processes:

- **Chaos (Klân):** Creation; forms emerge out of the Void.

- **Form (Chan):** Preservation; forms persist between Chaos and the Void.

- **Void (Dâr):** Destruction; forms dissolve into the Void.

Everything that exists cycles through these three states according to this progression:

Void → Creative Chaos → Form → Destructive Chaos → Void → ...

We call this progression the *klânchandâr kilûd* ("chaos-form-void cycle"). Black Sunnite strategists use this model to analyze a target and determine the best method of attack, based on whether the target's critical feature is Chaos, Form or Void. The idea is to destroy the target by moving it to the next state in the above cycle.

A Chaos target is a creative or destructive process that needs to be disrupted: an enemy Order, a rival business, a gang of vandals, etc. We attack a creative chaos target by introducing forms like ideologies, lawsuits or security forces that sap its creative energy. We attack a destructive chaos targets by moving it into the Void—i.e. arresting, killing and eradicating it.

A Form target is an orderly environment that we wish to disrupt. We attack Form by introducing Chaos; for example by lighting fires (physical or ideological), sounding false alarms, or spreading disinformation, doubt, fear and uncertainty in the enemy camp. This is the M.O. of the *Bor-Rûdor* ("Black Ninja"), who specializes in creating and exploiting chaos.

A Void target is an absence of something: a gap in a structure, a lack of perception, an absence of personnel or an ideological blind spot. We attack this void by creatively introducing a form into it: a Black Ninja hiding in the gap, a diversionary illusion or sound, a spy offering home improvement services at the target's estate, a new weaponized idea, etc.

THE TWO WORLDS

Dark Side metaphysics includes the very important concept of *Ârz Vor-Thûlz* ("The Two Worlds"), which are:

- **Formed World (Chanagum-Thûl):** Manifest, material world. Realm of stars, planets, plants, animals, objects; formed, nameable things. Physics.
- **Unformed World (Bulchanagum-Thûl):** Unmanifest, spiritual world. Realm of ideas, myths, universal laws; formless, unnameable things. Metaphysics.

Dark Side philosophy and spiritual practices seek to develop a powerful awareness of both worlds. Dark Side Sanctums and temples should have mandalas or symbols to represent each of these realms. Acolytes should meditate by gazing upon them, gaining awareness of and insight into both worlds. This is done to remind the Acolyte that he lives in both manifested and unmanifested realities, and should not become entirely absorbed in either at the expense of the other. If one is only aware of the formed world, one loses the ability to see through illusions of forms, perceive the flow of the Dark Tao, gather Bor-Zy and work magick. If one is too wrapped up in the unformed world, one becomes an impotent mystic, unable to impose one's will upon the material world or simply survive. For maximum power, one must have a foot in each world—one foot of a warrior and one foot of a mystic—and know how to connect the two worlds in one's own being.

Note that the klânchandâr model applies to both worlds; physical and metaphysical processes both follow the chaos-form-void cycle, so Dark Side strategists should always analyze a situation and attack a target in both world-dimensions according to this model.

Seeing the Shadow World

In Black Sunnite metaphysics we speak of a becoming a *Black Sun Seer (Borzûm-Gurûzâth):* one who learns to unsee the light of the White Sun that blinds most beings to the existence of the formless, Black Sunlit-world. The White Sunlight only illuminates *forms (chanz)*—those objects, ideas, words and social constructs we can conceive of, speak about and interact with. We say that the White Sun is the Source that fills our minds with models of the world—our mundane sensory awareness, plans, theories, philosophies, ideologies, religions, languages and cultures. To the White Sunnite, these constructs are all that one should be concerned about; anything outside of the White Sunlit-world is illusory, delusional, insignificant or evil. To the White Sunnite, "the map is the territory", outside of which he has no interest in venturing.

To the Black Sunnite, this situation is inverted. The map is not the extent of our world, but a "placid island of ignorance in the midst of black seas of infinity", to use H. P. Lovecraft's lovely phrase. It is the "black seas" beyond the borders of the map that are of interest, and toward which the Black Sunnite seeker sets sail. And it is the White Sunlit forms which are illusory, delusional, insignificant or evil—signifying as they do only the extent of our mental limitations and cultural conditioning. To discover a greater reality, the Black Sunnite looks into the shadows of the White Sunlit-world—and of his own mind.

Thus we have another way of describing the Two Worlds: the White Sunlit, formed world of *Mâlzamagum-Thûl ("White Sunlit-World")*, and the unlit, formless realm of *Borzamagum-*

Thûl ("Black Sunlit-World") or *Kâmûd-Thûl ("Shadow World")*. The White Sunlit-world is where almost all beings spend almost all of their time; the Shadow World is where only a few magicians, mystics, madmen and prophets dare to venture.

Other Descriptions of the Two Worlds

The dichotomy of the Two Worlds is an ancient metaphysical idea that appears in many traditions; below are some other descriptions of the Two Worlds from other traditions that show how universal this idea is:

- Castaneda's *Tonal* and *Nagual*.
- Plato's *Cave* and *world outside the Cave*.
- Hinduism's *Vyaktam* and *Avyaktam*.
- Shopenhauer's world as *Representation* and *Will*.
- Buddhism's *Taizokai (Womb World)* and *Kongokai (Diamond Realm)*.
- Kabbalism's *Ohr (Divine Light)* and *Ein Sof (the Infinite)*.
- Goedel's *Provable* and *Unprovable* theorems of mathematical logic.
- Taoism's *Ten Thousand Things* and *the Tao*.
- Kenneth Grant's *Universe A* and *Universe B*.
- Huxley's *ordinary mind* and *Mind at Large*.
- Islam's *Seen* and *Unseen* worlds.
- Shamanism's *World* and *Otherworld*.
- Kant's *Phenomenon* and *Noumenon*.
- Quantum Physics' *Observables* and *Wave Function*.

Our notion of Two Worlds is thus in general agreement with many other traditions, and is not particularly radical or strange. What is radical and strange are the dominant ideologies of this age of "Enlightenment", which posit a world that is only knowable through reason, language and sensory input, and which deprecate or deny the existence and power of any other world. It is this pervasive delusion that the Black Sun Seer must see through, but to do so requires a great deal of "unlearning" and "unseeing". For the mental constructs most of us have been conditioned with in this culture are designed to draw our attention only to the White Sunlit-world, leaving us totally blind to the existence of the Shadow World.

And this is why the perception of the Shadow World usually comes as such a shock and feels like such a cataclysm to those who experience it. It rends apart our conditioned inner landscape like an "unidentified mental object"—an intrusion from an alien world that threatens to destroy our own. It is this perception that we symbolize by the *Black Sun*: a portal to an incomprehensible outer dimension that we didn't previously suspect existed, suddenly opening before us, threatening to devour our inner space much as a black hole devours outer space. And this perception is what the initiated Black Sun Seer signifies by putting a black spot on his forehead between his eyes, marking him as one of those rare beings who has opened his *Third Eye (Zwot-Grâl)* to the existence of the Shadow World and now "walks under a Black Sun".

PHILOSOPHY OF DEATH

We dedicate a chapter to death because it is, in a sense, the only philosophical question that matters. If one's life ends soon in death, and one's entire existence is doomed to disappear into the Void without a trace, what possible value or meaning could anything one does in this life have? Here we discuss some possible answers to this age-old question at the heart of all philosophy, spirituality and religion.

Learning How to Die

The Roman philosopher Cicero wrote that "to philosophise is to learn how to die", and certainly one task of philosophy is to learn how to face death. But it is also to learn how to live in the face of death. For as a Taoist might observe, life and death are two poles of one phenomenon that cannot be separated; one cannot know life without knowing death, and vice versa. Each pole creates the other, as all things spring into existence from the fundamental "Tao" of "yin" and "yang" polarities. As Dark Taoists, we gravitate toward the "yin" or "Dark Side" of every polarity, so we are naturally more attracted to and fascinated by death than by life. Yet by studying death, even celebrating it, we may come to know life better than those who ignore or deny it.

The Primal Fear

The primal fear, which gives all other fear its force, is the fear of death. Why do we fear violent men, wild animals, pain, disease, the unknown?—ultimately, because they threaten us with death. The one who conquers his fear of death thus conquers all other fears. Overcoming this primal fear is the central task of the warrior, priest, doctor, mortician, philosopher and anyone else who faces death as a way of life.

To that end, various philosophers have attempted to persuade themselves by reason that death is nothing to fear; to rationalize it away or convince themselves that it is the beginning of authentic life. For example, the German philosopher Heidegger wrote:

> If I take death into my life, acknowledge it, and face it squarely, I will free myself from the anxiety of death and the pettiness of life—and only then will I be free to become myself.

How exactly one is to "face death squarely" then becomes the question. Can this be done by means of the rational mind, or does it require, as we claim, going "beneath" rational thought into the depths of the shadow-mind?

The philosopher Wittgenstein cleverly avoided this problem by denying death altogether:

> Death is not an event in life: we do not live to experience death. If we take eternity to mean not infinite temporal duration but timelessness, then eternal life belongs to those who live in the present. Our life has no end in the way in which our visual field has no limits.

According to Wittgenstein, death is not an experience, but the end of experience, whereas eternity *is* an experience—of timelessness. If we only concern ourselves with what we experience in the moment, then we are effectively immortal and death is of no concern. This is reminiscent of attitudes found in non-Western philosophies such as Zen, where methodologies for facing death have a long lineage.

The Way of the Samurai

In the East, the question of facing death has been addressed less intellectually by various schools of warrior philosophy. In his famous book of Samurai philosophy, *Hagakure*, author Tsunetomo writes that "the Way of the Samurai is found in death." He argues that the Samurai should choose death in any situation, and that to consider death a failure if it does not achieve one's aim is the "frivolous way of sophisticates." He goes on to describe the mindset toward death which the Samurai should cultivate, including a practical method for following Heidegger's advice to face death squarely:

> "Meditation on inevitable death should be performed daily. Every day when one's body and mind are at peace, one should meditate upon being ripped apart by arrows, rifles, spears and swords, being carried away by surging waves, being thrown into the midst of a great fire, being struck by lightning, being shaken to death by a great earthquake, falling from thousand-foot cliffs, dying of disease or committing seppuku at the death of one's master. And every day without fail one should consider himself as dead."

This is a powerful exercise that you won't find in any book of Western philosophy, but which we incorporate into our own Sith praxis (with minor updates, such as light sabers instead of swords, suns instead of fires, etc.)–see "Echelon Four Challenges". Note that one does not have to embrace the fatalistic Samurai view of death to benefit from this death meditation!

The Samurai philosophy of death would find its most potent manifestation in the 20th century, after the isolationist Samurai regime had been replaced by an Imperial regime that sought to beat the Western empires at their own colonial game. The "Dark Lords" of imperial Japan used Imperial Way Zen and Shinto ideology to motivate men to sacrifice themselves for their emperor by fighting stoically to the death or flying airplanes loaded with explosives into Allied ships. We see deadly echoes of this *kamikaze* philosophy today in the death-embracing philosophy of the Islamic suicide-bombers. As Sith, we do not follow such a path of self-sacrifice ourselves, but we are not adverse to encouraging others to do so if it serves both their purposes and our own. In any case, we must respect those who face death in this way, becoming instruments of conquest in the process, rather than merely philosophizing about it.

More Perspectives on Death

We now briefly discuss several more common perspectives on death from a Dark Side perspective.

Existentialism

"Existentialist" philosophers advocate living life with full awareness of death, as this gives the joys, choices and challenges of one's brief life their value. If your life never ended, your choices would have no value, just as the value of something in unlimited supply is zero.

This awareness manifests itself differently depending on whether one is an existentialist of the Light Side or the Dark Side. A Light Side existentialist might claim that we have a responsibility to "improve the world", to be kind to each other, or to simply enjoy the ride of life. A Dark Side existentialist might counter that death makes all attempts at world-improvement futile, that we are equally free to be cruel if we so desire, or that life is indeed a ride—straight into a black hole.

The Dark Side existentialist considers the Lightsider who puts a "happy face" on death to be as delusional as the death-denier who ignores it altogether. Both are taking their ride of life inside a spaceship with a virtual reality simulator playing 24/7 so they never have to see the black hole approaching outside the walls. A Dark Side existentialist prefers to take the ride in nothing but a space suit, looking straight at the black hole as it looms ever larger in his field of vision. The Dark Side existentialist who gazes into the black face of death is the only one seeing the ride for what it is. He may even find this face beautiful.

Gateway to the Afterlife

Another common philosophy of death is the one preached by most major religions: that death is not final, but a gateway to another world, another incarnation or another state of being. Life not an end in itself, but a test to be passed or an illusion to be transcended en route to one's eternal fate. "Near death experiences", communications with the deceased, "enlightened" states of consciousness, the teachings of prophets and memories of past lives are pointed to as evidence for the existence of a life after this one. Our attitude to these claims is one of skepticism, but interest. We consider life after bodily death an open question worthy of research. In particular, the possibility of directing one's reincarnation into another body via metaphysical or technological means is of keen interest, as we seek immortality for ourselves and our lineage.

Life Extension

An obvious way to deal with the problem of death is to seek to defeat it by material, scientific means. This approach goes back to the ancient Chinese emperors and Indian kings, who sought an "elixir of life" to extend their reigns, emplying armies of alchemists to test compounds containing minerals that were thought to extend life. Several emperors are thought to have been killed by these toxic elixirs, thus prematurely ending their quests for immortality.

In modern times, this quest continues—notably among "transhumanists" and "singularitarians", who are philosophically committed to the defeat of death and the unlimited expansion of intelligence and technology. This has led to the development of technologies such as cryogenics, whereby a would-be immortal pays a large sum of money to have his head removed at death and stored in a deep freeze tank indefinitely, in hopes that at some future date technology will be available to revive the person and transfer his brain to another container. Other technologies, such as genetic engineering, blood transfusions and "mind uploading" are being pursued by wealthy individuals with an age-old aversion to physical death who see no metaphysical alternative.

In the Galaxy Far, Far Away, the great Darth Plagueis was obsessed with defeating death by any means. But after extensive study of Sith and Jedi lore, he concluded that Force mysticism and faith in Sith legends were insufficient. So he undertook an intensive program of scientific research into the nature of life and the Force (some of it rather gruesome), to attempt to conquer death where mysticism failed. Plagueis developed a scientific theory of the Force by which he claimed he could create and extend life without resorting to the Force transference methods of his predecessors. Unfortunately, the laws of nature operate a bit differently in our galaxy, so it remains a challenge for future Sith scientists to unlock the secrets of physical immortality as Lord Plagueis did. But we can take inspiration from his fearless curiosity and willingness to reject millennia of tradition and superstition to arrive at a new, more powerful understanding of life.

The larger point here is that all these scientific attempts to extend life, from ancient history, currents events and legend, make perfect sense if one believes that death is a problem to be defeated, and this can only be achieved by material, technological means. But is that the case?

Mystical Immortality

Another response to the problem of death is to seek to transcend it by altering one's consciousness or working magick. Various mystical techniques may be employed, such as: meditations and yogas leading to a state of timeless awareness; use of psychedelic drugs to achieve the same; prayers or mantras that invoke a "divine mind" or sense of union with an eternal intelligence that transcends death; warrior training that puts one in a state where one experiences immortality in the present moment and no longer fears death; rituals that direct one's consciousness into another incarnation or the afterlife.

Buddhism is a prime exponent of the mystical approach. The Buddha taught that to escape the cycle of death and rebirth, one must achieve a "deathless" state of mind called *Nirvana*. He is recorded as telling a group of disciples: "Monks, remain with your minds well-established in these four establishings of mindfulness. Don't let the deathless be lost to you." Many advanced mystical techniques of the various Buddhist schools, from the Tibetan *Bardo* or "Great Liberation" rites designed to guide the Buddhist from the moment of death through the stages of reincarnation, to the Zen warrior practices of the Samurai that were designed to achieve the deathless state of mind.

In the Hindu tradition, there are holy men called *Aghoris* who dwell in charnel grounds, cover their bodies in crematoria ash and drink from skulls as part of their spiritual path. The purpose of these macabre practices is to achieve deathless consciousness; to liberate themselves from fear of death by transgressing taboos which are rooted in that fear; to realize the unity of all opposites, including life and death, and thus achieve unity of consciousness with the immortal god Shiva. This is another path of mystic immortality, which is thought to be the original "Left Hand Path" of liberation and immortality via transgression.

Since the Stone Age, shamans and sorcerers have worn skull masks, adorned themselves with bones, performed blood sacrifices and necromantic rites—to exploit the magickal power of death over the human imagination, but also to achieve a sense of immortality by attempting to command death with their magick. No Dark Side philosophy of death can be complete until it has faced the primeval fact of death's immense, irrational power over the human mind, nor until the philosopher has personally experienced the sense of immortality that can be gained via the mystical embrace of death. One task of the Dark Lord is to provoke such experiences in his Apprentices.

Nihilism

A common response to the problem of death is not to respond; to simply ignore the issue and live for today, pursuing one's interests while attempting to live in blissful ignorance of the spectre of the grim reaper who is coming to harvest your body, mind and soul. You may make elaborate plans for your short life, striving to get an education, have a successful career, a family, or what have you, without ever considering that it is all still going to end soon—perhaps today—at which point you will face the eternal Void with nothing to show for it. Such denial is a form of nihilism; you are denying that death has any meaning worth worrying about, and carrying on as if it is never going to come. In the modern world, this has become the default philosophy of death in fashionable society: eat, drink and be merry is the order of the day, while all talk of death is considered "negative", "dark", "depressing" and downright rude. Some may give death a bit of thought, conclude that it is inevitable, natural, and not worth worrying about, then go about their business of trying to forget about it. This attitude seems like no problem, until you are actually dying, at which point your death-denialism may turn into despair, panic or mortal terror.

The Dark Lords consider death-nihilism to be the most cowardly of all perspectives on death. By denying death you are denying life in the Taoist sense, failing to prepare for future terror, sacrificing the spiritual strength that comes from death-awareness, and limiting your horizons by never thinking outside the box of your fleeting material existence —the place where, in our view, the path to immortal greatness lies!

The Ozymandias and Invictus Paths

The conflict between a desire for unlimited life and acceptance of mortality is fundamental to the world's great myths, religions and philosophies. The religions of the "Right Hand Path" teach humility in life and acceptance of death as a gateway a greater existence in an afterlife. Among those who take a "Left Hand Path" of egotism and choose to be unbowed by death, there are different philosophies, two of which we call the "Ozymandias and Invictus Paths", after two great 19th century English Romantic poems that capture the passions of the two paths.

Ozymandias, by Percy Bysshe Shelley, mocks the pretensions of a mighty ancient king, whose quest for immortality has been reduced to ruins by the sands of time:

> I met a traveller from an antique land
> Who said: Two vast and trunkless legs of stone
> Stand in the desert... near them, on the sand,
> Half sunk, a shattered visage lies, whose frown,
> And wrinkled lip, and sneer of cold command,
> Tell that its sculptor well those passions read
> Which yet survive, stamped on these lifeless things,
> The hand that mocked them and the heart that fed;
>
> And on the pedestal these words appear:
> 'My name is Ozymandias, king of kings;
> Look on my works, ye Mighty, and despair!'
> Nothing beside remains. Round the decay
> Of that colossal wreck, boundless and bare
> The lone and level sands stretch far away.

Invictus, by William Ernest Henley, beautifully expresses the Sithy spirit of an unconquerable soul, who takes responsibility for his fate and faces the prospect of death without fear:

> Out of the night that covers me,
> Black as the pit from pole to pole,
> I thank whatever gods may be
> For my unconquerable soul.
>
> In the fell clutch of circumstance
> I have not winced nor cried aloud.
> Under the bludgeonings of chance
> My head is bloody, but unbowed.
>
> Beyond this place of wrath and tears
> Looms but the Horror of the shade,

And yet the menace of the years
Finds, and shall find me, unafraid.

It matters not how strait the gate,
How charged with punishments the scroll,
I am the master of my fate:
I am the captain of my soul.

Invictus ("Unconquered One") does not bow to death, but he doesn't deny it either; his attitude is similar to Dark Side existentialism we discussed earlier. But if Invictus goes further, seeking to immortalize himself with monuments to his glory, he becomes Ozymandias: the master of his fate becomes the sneering statue, decayed and abandoned in the desert. For surely every proud conqueror of the Left Hand Path is eventually humbled by the ineluctable power of time, entropy or gods of the Right Hand Path.

Does this mean the Dark Lord's quest for immortality is as futile as Ozymandias's? Not necessarily. For while cosmic forces do seek our humiliation and destruction, and will very like succeed, we can still live in the spirit of Invictus, "bloody, but unbowed". In each moment, in the "fell clutch of circumstance" of this doomed universe, do we not feel immortal when we adopt that fearless, indomitable spirit? And might we not yet find some way to defeat the forces that seek our destruction if, rather than submitting fatalistically to them, we fight them to our last breath? This is the faith of the Sith Lord and other disciples of the Left Hand Path, who seek unlimited power and immortality, and in that seeking, may find it.

The Tao of Death

To a Dark Taoist, death is just another manifestation of the yin-yang (in-yo) polarities that define reality. To die is to follow the flow of the Tao; it is as futile to fight death as to fight the fact that night follows day. Fujiybayashi makes this point well in the classic Ninjutsu text *Bansenshukai*:

> As a year has spring and winter, in spring trees and plants grow while in winter they conceal themselves, the sun and the moon rise and set, a day has day and night, the man wakes or sleeps, lives or dies. Spring is *yo* and of life, while winter is *in* and of death. Also, moonrise is *yo* while sunset or moonset is *in* and a man's waking state is *yo* while sleeping is *in*. This means that to live is *yo* while to die is *in*. If you hate and fear to die young, why would you not hate or dread winter to come, or the sun and the moon to set, night to fall or a man to sleep? As sleep is a small part of *in*, so death is a large form of *in*. What is the reason you hate only death but do not hate to sleep? You should be ready to die with nothing to fear.

To put it in Black Sunnite language, if one embraces the Dark Side of all things, then surely one must embrace death, which is the Dark Side of life, rather than resist it. To "rage, rage against the dying of the Light", as the poet put it, is to cling to the fleeting rays of the White Sun and resist walking fully under the Black Sun in death. This is not the way of our kind.

Life in Death, Death In Life

There is another aspect of the Tao of death, which we call "Life in Death, Death in Life" ("*Gâth âg Mâzûk, Mâz âg Gâthûk*"). This is an application of a Dark Taoist principle, that whenever you seek one thing you bring about its opposite. If you have a mentality of fearing death and wanting only to survive, you are in fact more likely to die. Conversely, if you have a "devil may care" attitude, thinking of yourself as already dead, knowing that whatever happens is the will of the Dark Tao, feeling that you have nothing to lose, you will have a great advantage over enemies who fear death. You will find as you embrace death that you come alive; you will awaken instinctive powers held in check by your death-fearing mind; you will not hesitate and you will not be shocked or demoralized by events. Therefore, you will be more likely to continue to live.

We can remind ourselves of this principle by writing it in the Hârzad script in our sanctums and temples:

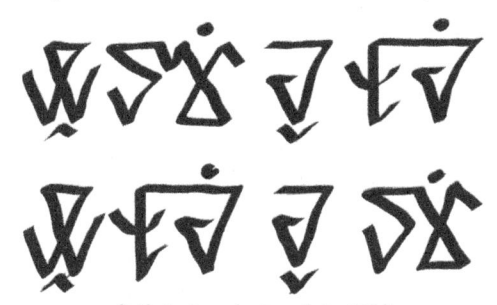

{Life in Death, Death in Life}

Memento Mori

The Dark Side disciple should keep certain symbols at hand—black suns, skulls, black robes, etc.—as reminders that he will die. Indeed, these symbols are a reminder that everything in existence—ourselves, our friends and families, our tribes, our races, our civilizations, our species, our planet, our sun, our galaxy, our entire universe—is doomed to destruction. As the ancient Chinese sages said, when asked for a saying that is true in all times and places: "this, too, shall pass". Nothing in this world is eternal. The fate of everything is Darkness. Nothing can escape its destiny in the Void of the Black Sun.

Unlike the modern Lightsider who lives in denial and mortal fear of this reality, the Darksider embraces it, takes dark inspiration from it, reminds himself of it often and pays tribute to it by his devotion to symbols of death such as the Black Sun. Thus do we revive the ancient tradition of "memento mori"—the practice of keeping death imagery at hand as a reminder of our mortality—common since ancient times but forgotten in the modern age. We use these symbols not simply as gloomy reminders, but to glorify the power of death, universal destruction and ourselves as dead men walking under the Black Sun. We also use them as a challenge to ourselves, to always strive to achieve immortality and defeat death before it defeats us.

The Brotherhood of Death

> "Everyone wants to be foremost in this future-and yet death and the stillness of death are the only things certain and common to all in this future! How strange that this sole thing that is certain and common to all, exercises almost no influence on men, and that they are the furthest from regarding themselves as the brotherhood of death!"
>
> "My death I praise to you, the free death that comes to me because I want. And when will I want it? — Whoever has a goal and an heir wants death at the right time for his goal and heir. And out of reverence for his goal and heir he will no longer hang withered wreaths in the sanctuary of life." —Friedrich Nietzsche

Death can be considered the culmination of life; the climactic chapter of one's story that gives it a greater meaning, power and resonance for the ages. A great death means living on in the minds of others as a hero or martyr, thus becoming a source of Force for others who will gain inspiration from a great death that they never would have from an ordinary one. Death can thus serve greater power, if it is achieved at the right time and in the right way so as to enhance one's legacy and cause.

In the Galaxy Far, Far Away, the Sith Lords under the Baneite Rule of Two made great death a key tool of their cult's power. Each Master expected and accepted that he would meet death at the hands of his Apprentice when the latter was powerful enough to assume leadership of the Order. Thus did the Sith put their philosophy into practice: the Master in effect sacrifices himself for the ideal of "might is right", by requiring the Apprentice to kill him and thus prove his right to rule and continue the Sith lineage. In this way, each Sith Lord's death give birth to a new Lord—another link in the immortal chain of power called Dark Lordship. In death, the Sith Lord proved that his life, for all its selfish pursuit of power, was ultimately a selfless pursuit of a higher ideal: the immortal power of the Sith Order and the Dark Side. We advocate a similar methodology for our Sith "brotherhood of death" in this universe, at this time.

Death Worship

Perhaps the most extreme philosophy of death is to consider death itself a source of Force power, an object of spiritual devotion or even of worship. The death-worshipper essentially waves the white flag (or the black flag) in his battle against onrushing death, and instead of seeking a way to defeat it, fully embraces and celebrates it. Death, rather than being seen as the ultimate "evil" for negating life, consciousness and happiness, is seen as an ultimate "good"—either because it negates the suffering of life, or because one is anti-life for some other reason and is pleased to see it end. Death is not defeat and the dying of the Light to the death-worshipper, but deliverance into eternal Darkness. When the spirit of "memento mori" goes beyond "remember that you must die" to "celebrate that you must die", or even "consider yourself as already dead", it becomes a macabre, anti-life philosophy. Yet it is one that can be defended.

Throughout history, men have expressed their awe at the power of death by their fealty to various death deities, and their willingness to sacrifice living beings to them. This impulse is inherent in man; no amount of "enlightenment", "progress" or religious indoctrination seems capable of preventing human beings from embracing the spirit of death worship eventually. We see this is every culture down thought history to our own, as individuals, groups and entire societies have periodically embraced death as a spiritual end in itself. In fact we appear to be living through such a time right now, as vampires, gothic sensibilities, macabre entertainments, anti-natalist ideologies, suicide terrorism and death-worshipping cults such as Santa Muerte have become popular cultural phenomena.

Death-worship is a subject of keen interest to the Dark Lords. In our book *Black Templar Handbook,* we describe a human sacrifice rite that is an example of death-worship for the purpose of invoking Force in the sacrificers. In *Sith Academy: Acolyte Training* we described a cult of assassins called the *Black Circle* who worship death as a deity and see in assassination an act of offering to their Death-God, who will bestow favors upon them in proportion to the importance of the person killed. Taken to its extreme, the death-worshipper may become a kind of spiritual vampire, who glorifies death, imagines himself to already be dead, and seeks the death of others so they may join him in the experience of anti-life. The Dark Lords will explore the darker extremes of death philosophy at greater length in a book called *The Vampire Handbook,* to be published at a future date by Black Temple Publishing.

PHILOSOPHY OF HISTORY, POLITICS AND EMPIRE

Now we turn to Dark Side philosophy as it applies to large scale human social constructs—cultures, nations, civilizations, races, and narratives of history.

Philosophy of History

History, to a Dark Lord, is a collection of stories of past glories to take inspiration from and defeats to learn from. It is a grand stage where metaphysical currents play out, philosophies are put to their hardest test, and men are challenged to be great or be ground under its wheels. We seek to understand history so that we may command it rather than be crushed by it, connect to ancient lineages of power, and conceive new chapters of glory that have yet to be written.

Progress and Cycles

The modern Western mind is infatuated with models of linear "progress", according to which history is ever-evolving toward a state of greater knowledge, enlightenment, justice, prosperity, etc. These models are usually given a moralistic slant, with slogans such as "the arc of the universe is long, but it bends toward justice". In this view, the progressive process not only brings material improvement, but moral and spiritual betterment over everything that came before. For believers in the "religion of progress", this way of thinking results in the dismissal of almost the entirety of human history as one long tale of woe, ignorance and darkness; it is "a nightmare from which we are trying to awaken". In the progressive view, history has nothing to teach us but how good we are compared to everything that came before us, and what we must avoid repeating.

Another way of viewing history, which was common before the rise of progressive philosophy, was that civilizations developed according to cycles of rise and fall, civility and barbarism, strength and weakness, knowledge and ignorance, virtue and corruption, order and chaos, ascent and decadence, etc. For example, Hindus posited the existence of a cycle of four great ages, or *yugas*, which begins with a golden age of truth, virtue and health and steadily degenerates until the fourth age, the *Kali Yuga*, which is marked by universal corruption, destruction, disease, ignorance and environmental destruction (Hindus believe we are currently in the Kali Yuga, and it won't end for another 427,000 years!) Less metaphysically, the Arab historian Ibn Khaldun theorized that history moves according to cycles of tribal vitality and civilized decadence. In this model, as tribes settle into urban living and lose their tribal solidarity and vitality, they grow soft, divided and weak. This allows more vital, cohesive tribes to conquer them and establish a new regime. But eventually the conquering tribe succumbs to the same decadence, is overthrown by another tribe, and the cycle repeats.

There is a slogan that captures the essence of such cyclical philosophies of history:

> Good times make weak men
> Weak men make hard times

> Hard times make strong men
> Strong men make good times

This is a simple, common-sensical slogan, but also a dagger in the heart of the progressive project, for it suggests that all our efforts to make good times will eventually produce the opposite. In fact this is a Taoist argument, because it recognizes that one extreme contains and causes the other extreme: there is darkness within light, and light within darkness. It is impossible to ever vanquish all darkness or progress forever in one direction, as progressive metaphysics would have it. In Lao-Tzu's words: "Fill your bowl to the brim and it will spill. Keep sharpening your knife and it will blunt."

The Dark Tao of History

What of the Sith? Are we historical progressives or cyclicalists? The answer is both. There are aspects of progressivism that the Sith do endorse; we have already discussed "evilution", and the idea that humanity is "progressing" toward a greater state—not of greater "morality" or "goodness" in the Judeo-Christian sense, but of greater *knowledge, power* and *evil*. We may also be progressing toward post-humanity: toward life forms that will resemble demons or dark demigods to normal humans. But this process of evilution is surely not bending toward greater justice, in the slave moralist sense of greater equality and more power for weak beings vis-a-vis the strong. That is simply not written into the laws of this universe, by whatever forces or dark gods brought it into being. In a war universe such as this one, "progress" equates to "that which brings power and victory". So evilution is a form of progress, though it is one that most progressives of today find repugnant. How unfortunate for them.

However, the Sith also hold to a "regressive" understanding of history, in that we recognize that everything in existence is slowly dying out, crumbling to dust, burning out, going dark and returning to the Void from whence it came. Entropy and darkness rule this universe, according both to intuition and the findings of science. What possible progress can there be in such a universe, in the ultimate analysis? Some progress can occur, even on a long time scale, but it cannot go on forever. Eventually the Darkness will return, things will fall apart, and everything will return to the Void from whence it came. We call this perspective "Dark Taoism", because it recognizes the possibility of linear progression, but only within the larger yin-yang cycle of rise and fall, with everything ultimately returning to the primordial Darkness as driven by the natural laws or "Dark Tao" of this universe.

Commandeering History

The Sith do not take a purely fatalistic view of history like a Hindu, a slave moralistic view like a monotheist, or a mundane materialist view like a Marxist. Rather, we take a *Black Magician's* view: that the trajectory of history can be bent to our Force-inflamed black magickal wills. We seek unlimited power so that we may *commandeer* history rather than become its victims. We seek to write the history books as the victors, rather than being written out of them as the losers. Even now, with each book we publish, we are writing the history of the future, and thereby stamping our imaginations and wills upon events that have yet to unfold. For our kind always look to the future, toward the culmination of history that we create and call *the Empire*.

We must always stay flexible in our machinations, recognizing that different strategies will be necessary depending on which stage a civilization is in in its rise-and-fall cycle. If it is in a late, declining stage, we may work to accelerate the degenerative trends, thus hastening the onset of the civilization's collapse and the end of the age, rather than trying to build our castle upon a crumbling foundation. In such cases, the Sith may act as revolutionaries, spiritual arsonists, civilizational vandals—lighting fires in the hearts and minds of men that will burn the decrepit order to the ground. Under more favorable regimes, we may operate in a more constructive manner, working within the system, molding its leaders minds, becoming part of the power-that-be, until we have accumulated enough influence that we can openly push events decisively toward the establishment of the Empire. This is where a keen perception of historical cycles and metaphysical forces is so important to our kind. Because our project spans many lifetimes and entire ages, we must always be aware of where we are in the historical timeline. We must then take the actions appropriate to our time to move the timeline forward, toward the day when we become the "right men at the right time" rather than a delusional cult waiting for a day that never comes.

Magick and Empire

Science vs. Magick

Anyone subscribing to a magickal philosophy, as the Dark Lords do, while simultaneously having ambitions of power, must have an answer to this question: if magick is so powerful, why are societies where magickal thinking is prevalent so poor and weak? Why is Haiti, land of Voudon, the poorest country in the Western hemisphere? How did China conquer Tibet—land of the legendary lama-magicians—and how do they continue to occupy and Han-ize it? What power does magick have against modern science, technology and industry? Isn't magick really a superstition left over from a pre-scientific age that keeps societies that believe in it backwards and powerless?

In the first place, it is wrong to describe modern, Western, scientific civilization as non-magickal. Magick is everywhere in this civilization, but it takes forms that many don't recognize as such: advertising, films, political slogans, popular music, infomercials, hypno-therapy, internet memes, etc. The people engaging in these activities for the purposes of acquiring power and influence are magicians, regardless of what they call themselves. In fact, the pervasiveness of these techniques in modern society suggest that this could be the most magickal society in history—a de facto Magocracy, in which the "invisible governors" who can best manipulate media, money and opinions are the real rulers, regardless of who holds high offices and wins elections.

Many may not find this modern Magocracy very magickal, because it lacks an overt metaphysical ideology. There seems to be no over-arching metaphysical goal in modern civilization—just a program of mundane wealth accumulation, technological advancement, increased lifespans and other improvements in utilitarian measures of "progress". In other words, we have a regime that uses magickal means to pursue mundane goals; if there is a deeper metaphysical purpose to this regime's magick, it keeps it rather concealed—perhaps restricted to an occulted "Illuminati"—and doesn't reveal it to the masses. There are attempts to make technologies such as space exploration, global communications, transhumanist engineering and artificial intelligence the basis for a scientific metaphysics of evolution toward a higher state of being for individuals and humanity as a whole—a "Singularity" or "Omega Point"—but this has yet to really take hold and replace older metaphysical systems such as monotheism. We have previously written about the "Force starvation crisis" that this lack of a higher metaphysical motivator—what we call a *Source*—creates for modern humans. It remains a great problem for scientific civilization, and a challenge for the magicians of the world, to step up and offer bold new metaphysical visions, and thereby become the highest guides for humanity and the wielders of ultimate power. This is how the present imbalance between magick and science can be righted, and magicians can take their rightful places as the triumphant masters of scientific civilization rather than its defeated enemies.

There is no better example of the triumph of the magicians over science than in the Star Wars universe, where the great Sith Lords Sidious and Vader engineered a coup that brought the most powerful black magicians in the galaxy to power, in short order building two great Death Stars and restoring the greatness of the Galactic Empire. This is an inspiring model of magick and science working together going forward, and a vision toward which all Sith should direct their imaginations, wills and Force power!

Morning of the Black Magicians

> Inexorably, hesitantly, terrible as fate, the great task and question is approaching: how shall the earth as a whole be governed? And to what end shall 'man' as a whole—and no longer as a people, a race—be raised and trained? —Friedrich Nietzsche, *The Will to Power*

It is our perception as Dark Lords that the political regimes that dominate the present age have reached a point of exhaustion, stagnation and bankruptcy, and are overdue for a great upheaval. In particular, we believe the regime of "liberal democracy" that gained ascendancy with the rise of Anglo-American civilization in the 18th century is approaching the end of its reign, and will soon be eclipsed by stronger alternatives. Which alternatives prevail has yet to be decided; whether it is techno-fascistic super-states, anarcho-capitalist chaos, traditionalist empires, collapse into a global dark age, or something else, will be decided on the battlefields of history. The important point for us is that we are entering an era of systems failure, when old regimes and ideologies have lost much of their appeal and credibility, and the future looks increasingly uncertain. This means that societies will be open to alternatives they were unwilling to consider before, and grand opportunities for men with new ideas, vision, boldness and iron will will be available where they previously hadn't been. We speak of the "morning of the Black Magicians": a time when those who dare to dream of greatness and empire may rise from obscurity, as Dark Lords have done throughout history, to stamp our wills upon the world with heavy boots and make our marks with iron fists. But first we must have a clear vision and a potent philosophy—boots and fists will come later.

A Dark Side Declaration of Independence

Our first intellectual act must be to reject the ruling creeds of this age and offer a more potent alternative. Thomas Jefferson, the key architect of the American Revolution that initiated a new age of Enlightenment-informed political regimes across the world, stated his creed at the outset of the "Declaration of Independence", emphasizing equality, "inalienable rights" endowed by a "creator", and "life, liberty and the pursuit of happiness". We, who declare our independence from these mundane Enlightenment regimes and seek to initiate a new age of Endarkenment, Empire and magick across this planet, offer the following "Dark Side

Declaration of Independence":

> We hold these truths to be self-evident: that all men are created evil; that they are endowed by the Dark Side with certain insatiable lusts; that among these are myth, vitality and the pursuit of power. To harness these lusts for the greatness and glory of all, an Empire shall be instituted across this planet and beyond, which derives it authority from the Dark Side of the Force, and embodies it in the wills of the Dark Lords.

Thus do we make clear from the outset that our project of Empire is radically different from the dominant regimes of the present age, and in effect make a declaration of war upon them. Let us now turn to the question of what political form our imperial regime might take.

Ruling Systems

As the Sith begin to plant the seeds of our Empire in the minds of others, we must consider which form of government will be most amenable to our aims. The following are several governmental forms that we find promising, and which Sith Acolytes should be familiar with. Which ruling system our Empire ultimately adopts will depend on the inclinations of the Dark Lords, the historical circumstances and the will of the Dark Side.

Magocracy

Magick has famously been defined as "the art and science of causing change to occur in conformity with the Will", which is another way of saying that magick is the art and science of wielding power. It follows that magicians, as the masters of magick, are those who are most worthy of wielding power in any society. Just as you would expect doctors of medicine to lead surgeries and attorneys in law to lead legal proceedings, magicians should be leading society at is highest level, using their knowledge of ritual, symbols, myths and human psychology to motivate, manipulate and command their people. Rule by magicians, or *magocracy*, is thus a natural and ancient form of government, going back to the shaman-chiefs, god-emperors and priest-kings of the ancient world.

Our political project as Sith is to restore the ancient magocratic system to its rightful place, elevating the magicians to their natural position as the ruling caste and displacing the technocrats, plutocrats and demagogues who have usurped them in this aberrant democratic age. In place of the French Republican triad of *"Liberty, Equality, Fraternity"* we shall raise the Sith Imperial triad of *"Power, Magic, Will"* as the motto of our new magocratic age.

Kratocracy

Kratocracy is rule by the strong; a "might is right" system in which the legitimate rulers are those who are strong and bold enough to seize and hold power. In a sense, kratocracy encompasses all governments, because the bare fact that any government is in power makes it a legitimate kratocracy. However, what is meant here are regimes that glorify their might above other values, and assert that their ability to seize power makes them ipso facto the best rulers of a society. A kratocracy isn't beholden to ideals such as "favor of the gods", "progress", "prosperity" or "tradition"; it may be leftist or rightist, populist or oligarchic; the only ideological principle it requires is "might makes right".

Kratocracy will certainly be a viable option for our Empire

going forward, once we can command the armies and allegiances necessary to overthrow the existing regimes and seize power. It is perfectly consistent with our philosophical Pillars, particularly The Primacy of Power and The Tao of Darwin. Internally, our Order functions largely as a kratocracy, in which those who seize power are respected as the legitimate ruling Dark Lords. However, for the external Imperial regime a more complex ideological foundation may be preferable—one that better reflects the depth and majesty of our Zithodûn philosophy, and which is more likely to win over the hearts and minds that matter.

Kreissocracy

Kreissocracy, from the Greek word *kreisson*, meaning "superior", is a term coined by the Dark Lords to refer to a government by superior beings. In a kreissocracy, the ruler may be a single "God-Emperor" or "Messiah", or an oligarchy of Supermen. The rulers may be the best of humanity, or even members of a new species of *homo superior*, possessing superhuman powers of intelligence, strength, psychic ability, etc. An inspiring example of a science-fictional kreissocracy was the regime of the *Augments*, led by Khan Noonien Singh, from the *Star Trek* universe. Augments possessed five times the strength and twice the intelligence as ordinary humans, and almost succeeded in conquering Earth during the "Eugenics Wars" of the late twentieth century.

The fifth Pillar of Sith philosophy contends that men are in the process of becoming Supermen, and that Sith should work to accelerate this evolution. It stands to reason that, if and when they emerge, such Supermen will become the natural rulers of the world. But the world has not yet seen a true kreissocracy because, as Nietzsche observed:

> Never yet has there been a Superman. Naked I saw

both the greatest and the smallest man. They are still all-too-similar to each other. Verily even the greatest I found all-too-human.

So kreissocracy remains a political system for the future and a goal to strive for. As in the Star Wars universe, where the Empire was ruled by true Supermen in the form of Sith Lords, so our Empire should be ruled by beings who have made themselves greater than men by the power of the Dark Side.

Theocracy

Theocracy is rule by a religious Order, such as the Catholic church or the Tibetan lamacracy. Theocracy is similar to a magocracy, in that priesthoods and magical orders use similar methods to assert and maintain their power. The primary difference is that theocracy employs sources of traditional religious authority such as prophetic revelations, divine guidance, sacred texts, symbols and rituals, whereas a magocracy is more creative, less dogmatic and need not invoke gods or prophets to assert its authority.

The Empire of Star Wars was essentially a Dark Side theocracy, with Darth Sidious acting as the Pope and Darth Vader as the vice-Pope. While their religious ideology was never described in detail, the Star Wars-era Sith clearly had a strong faith in the Dark Side that drove them and made them hostile to non-believers—as Darth Vader made clear when he told Admiral Motti menacingly: "I find your lack of faith disturbing..."

In our universe, we envision the Empire having theocratic elements, which may vary depending on the Sources followed by the ruling Dark Lords. For example, Darth Imperius is a devotee of the Black Sun Source, and has developed the ideology for a religion of "Black Sunnism", which could very well become the basis for the imperial "black theocracy" of the future.

Apotheocracy

Apotheocracy is a term we are coining for rule by a "god-emperor" or "divine king". Apotheocracy is one of the most ancient and powerful ruling systems, combining as it does the strengths of monarchy and theocracy. Under this system, the ruler is thought to be a divine being—an incarnate god or a "chosen one" who directly channels the will and spirit of the gods. Examples of apotheocracies include the regimes of the Egyptian Pharaohs (incarnations of Horus), Chinese emperors ("Sons of Heaven"), Roman emperors ("Divi Filii"—"Sons of God"), Hindu god-kings ("Devarajas"), medieval Popes, Tibetan Dalai Lamas and Japanese Emperors ("Arahitogami"). An awesome fictional example of an apotheocratic ruler was Sauron in the Third Age of Middle Earth, who was revered as a dark god-king by those who fell under his spell.

We foresee that our own Empire will in time evolve into such an apotheocracy, when Dark Lords of sufficient power and mystique appear who can demonstrate their god-like nature. We have already had visions of such a regime: a *Black Sun Empire* ruled by a *Black Emperor*—the "Son of the Shadow", who is believed to be the avatar of the Black Sun itself during his reign. More about our dark apotheocratic visions will be forthcoming in future publications.

Caste System

Traditionally, human civilizations have been divided into four hierarchical classes or castes: farmers/slaves, merchants/bourgeoisie, warriors/aristocrats, and priests/spiritual elites. In a traditional order, power flows downward from the spiritual elite, whose myths define the highest values of the civilization, guide the lords and inspire the warriors. The warrior-aristocrats in turn protect and expand the wealth of the bourgeoisie, while receiving their technical support. The bourgeoisie in turn manage and patronize the farmers and slaves. We can observe this pattern from the earliest known civilizations all the way to our present postmodern societies, regardless of which political system holds power. If there is a natural human social order, this quadripartite caste system is surely it.

In our modern age of industrial democracy, we can characterize the four castes as follows:

- Slaves: low-wage laborers, welfare dependents (wage class)
- Bourgeoisie: small businessmen, corporate employees, mid-level government employees (salary class)
- Aristocracy: industrialists, corporate, political and military elite (investor class)
- Spiritual Leaders: cultural and intellectual elites, religious leaders

Note that the activities of the four castes in modern society are somewhat different than in traditional feudal societies, due primarily to recent technological and economic developments. For example, the slave caste is no longer mostly peasant farmers, since agriculture requiers only a small fraction of the modern labor force. The equivalent today are all the low wage laborers and welfare recipients, who are totally dependent on their employers, have few prospects for upward mobility, no net worth and no power in society. The priest caste is no longer just religious leaders, as religion has lost much of its power since the onset of the secular Enlightenment in the 18th century. Now a mixed bag of cultural elites, celebrities, gurus, religious leaders and intellectuals share the task of guiding and inspiring their societies as priesthoods once did.

The Dark Lords recognize the lasting power of this four caste system, and don't seek to overthrow it. In fact we seek to restore it, as we recognize that in the modern world this order has become distorted, such that warriors and spiritual leaders are now subservient to merchants and industrialists when they should command them. In our imperial caste system, the spiritual caste we call the Dark Lords will reign supreme, followed by the warrior caste, then the industrialists, bourgeoisie and laborers. No caste will be denigrated and all will be treated with respect, but this is the time-tested social order that in our view best maximizes the Force power of all.

Fascism

Many of our preferred ruling systems might be characterized as forms of *fascism* by people of this era, who use it as a catch-all term for illiberal political systems they disapprove of. Fascism is indeed a political philosophy of keen interest to the Dark Lords, as one of the most potent modern attempts to manifest Dark Side values in the political sphere. Let us now discuss a few forms of fascism that have particularly informed our Dark Side political philosophy.

Imperial Way Zen

In 1868, the Meiji Restoration put the Emperor on the highest seat of Japanese power, restoring imperial rule after seven centuries of rule by the *Shoguns*, or Samurai warlords.

Japan was already fascistic, in the kratocratic sense of being ruled by the strongest military factions, but post-Meiji it became more imperially and mystically inclined. An ideology was created called "Imperial Way Zen" that merged Zen Buddhism with the Emperor-reverence that was part of Japan's traditional religion of Shinto. Under this regime, Buddhists were expected to show their loyalty to the Emperor, and the traditional Japanese samurai code of *Bushido ("way of the warrior")* gained favor over the more pacifistic teachings of the Buddha. Zen monks trained high-ranking military men in methods of developing steel-hard wills and stoic attitudes toward suffering and death. The result was a ferocious warrior elite that achieved a string of victories and rapidly established a formidable empire across East Asia.

Under Imperial Way Zen, revered monks emphasized the martial virtues of Zen. For example, D. T. Suzuki wrote:

> The soldierly quality, with its mysticism and aloofness from worldly affairs, appeals to the Willpower. Zen in this respect walks hand in hand with the spirit of Bushido.

Harada Sogaku, creator of what he called "war Zen", showed a Sithy awareness of the War Universe when he wrote:

> In all phenomena of either the ordinary world or the spiritual world, there is not one where war is absent. How could Zen alone be free of this principle? ... It is impermissible to forget war for even an instant.

Imperial Way Zen was a fascinating attempt to fuse a mystical lineage, a warrior ethos and an imperial hierarchy into a potent system of rule and conquest. Those looking for models for a Sith Empire from this planet's history would do well to study the ideology of Imperial Japan. The Japanese empire might have gone on to conquer Asia had they not been impatient and unfortunate enough to encounter another expansionist empire at the peak of its power: the United States of America.

Synarchism

Synarchism is the inverse of anarchism or primitive communism: rather than a non-hierarchical society with no rulers, it advocates rule by a small elite. It originated with a 19th century French occultist named Alexandre Saint-Yves, who sought a system where "illuminated" secret societies with metaphysical agendas could wield controlling influence over the levers of political power. Synarchists were early supporters of the European fascist movements, which they hoped would create the kind of hierarchical, illuminated order they sought. Synarchism has been a guiding ideology behind the European Union project for almost a century, though its influence remains largely unknown. It has strong ties to Freemasonry—most notably the *Propaganda Due* (P2) Italian Lodge that attempted a Synarchist coup and controlled a covert European army that conducted terrorist operations and plotted right wing coups as part of *Operation Gladio* in the 1970s and 80s. The Synarchist project is still ongoing today, with fascistic groups such as ISIS and Ukrainian militias showing the hallmarks of Synarchist sponsorship in the tradition of Gladio.

Synarchism has been strongly inspired by Nietzschean philosophy, according to which there is a small class of Supermen who are the rightful rulers of civilization. These Supermen are free to operate "beyond good and evil"— outside the moral values of the common people, as they must to successfully rule. Synarchism has philosophical roots going back to Plato, who advocated a society ruled by an elite of "Philosopher-Kings" who propagated "noble lies" to the masses to enable civilization to function. In practice, Synarchism is essentially global corporatism, in which international industrialists, secret societies and private armies seek to subvert national governments and establish larger power structures such as the European Union and the so-called "New World Order". The Dark Lords consider Synarchism to be one of the most intriguing and impressive attempts to implement a Sith-like order on this planet to date, though we would like to see something darker and more militant still.

Mystical Fascism

Mystical fascism is a general term for a regime of poets, sorcerers and warriors: an ideology driven by power, passion, vitality, myth, magick and mysticism. It is the polar opposite of the sterile, technocratic "liberalism" that dominates the present age, which gives it the flavor of a potent but forbidden fruit. Mystical fascism aligns well with the type of Black Magocracy envisioned by the Dark Lords, being consonant with our philosophy of Force hierarchy, unfettered will to power and black magickal "might is right".

Mystical fascism unleashes forces from the Shadow-mind that compel men to march to war for their god-emperor, prophet or people. It is extremely potent, as shown by the blitzkrieg conquests of the early Muslims and the Axis powers, but it has a tendency to self-destruct in an orgy of violence. If it succeeds, mystical fascism can become the ideological basis of a new empire that lasts for centuries.

In our view, secular liberal ideologies will always fall eventually to mystical fascism, because they starve vital aspects of the mind and soul that humans crave. Men will never be content with merely materialistic, hedonistic, rationalist, economic and political ideologies. We crave myth, magic, gods and leaders who can connect us to something transcendent. George Orwell understood this well back in 1940, when mystical fascism was at the peak of its power and appeal, when he wrote:

> [Hitler] has grasped the falsity of the hedonistic attitude to life. Nearly all western thought since the last war, certainly all "progressive" thought, has assumed tacitly that human beings desire nothing beyond ease, security and avoidance of pain. In such a view of life there is no room, for instance, for patriotism and the military virtues. ... Hitler ... knows that human beings don't only want comfort, safety, short working-hours, hygiene, birth-control and, in general, common sense; they also, at least intermittently, want struggle and self-sacrifice, not to mention drums, flags and loyalty-parades. However they may be as economic theories, Fascism and Nazism are psychologically far sounder than any hedonistic conception of life. ... Whereas Socialism, and even capitalism in a more grudging way, have said to people "I offer you a good time," Hitler has said to them "I offer you struggle, danger and death," and as a result a whole nation flings itself at his feet.

Orwell's words about Hitler and the appeal of Nazism apply just as well today to ISIS, various "alt-right" groups, and indeed our own project of Sithism. Will the world be plunged into another great war to satisfy the hunger for struggle, danger and death that gnaws at the soul of liberal civilization? It seems quite likely.

COSMIC PHILOSOPHY

One of our great philosophical interests as galactic imperialists is to orient ourselves within the larger cosmos. We ask and seek answers to questions such as: What is the Sith's relationship to the larger universe? What is our purpose within it? What should be our actions and attitude toward it? In this chapter we present some possible answers to these questions.

THE FOUR COSMIC SCHOOLS

The Dark Lords have identified four schools of thought of interest in orienting ourselves in the cosmos, which we briefly summarize below.

Cosmism:

- The universe is a means to unlimited power, immortality and godhood.
- Goals: Explore, exploit and conquer the universe for our own glory.
- Examples: Sithism, Singularitarianism

Acosmism:

- The universe is an illusion; nothing exists.
- Goals: See through the illusion; disentangle one's mind from the illusory web of matter and sensory

perception.

- Examples: Buddhism, Sunyata school of Hinduism

Anti-Cosmism:

- The universe is a vast prison and a horrible mistake.
- Goals: Oppose the creator gods and Cosmist ideologies; work to destroy the universe.
- Examples: Anti-Cosmic Satanism, Black Sunnism

Cosmicism:

- The universe is alien, indifferent and incomprehensible.
- Goals: Abandon reason, sanity and the pursuit of knowledge. Flee into insanity and ignorance.
- Example: Cthulhu Cults, Nihilism

We now discuss each cosmic school of thought in more detail.

COSMISM

{ Before Darth Imperius turned to the Dark Side and began propagating his vision of Sithism, he was an aficionado of science fiction and an avid proponent of space exploration. He studied space science, read the works of visionary futurists, and eventually developed an entire philosophy, ideology and "space religion" which he called *Cosmism*. Sithism has in many respects evolved out of that vision, as his reflections and revelations about man and the Cosmos led him to a darker vision of human nature and potential within this universe. This section is based on his earlier work on Cosmism; Sithism, so far as it relates to the larger Cosmos and the Galactic Empire, could be called "Dark Cosmism" or "Sith Cosmism". }

The Call of the Cosmos

The essence of Cosmism is a sense of awe at the potential for unlimited power that exists out in the universe. The Cosmist looks to the vast cosmos as a challenge to himself and others to *evolve*—toward a more powerful state of consciousness, civilization, imagination and material mastery. For the Sith Cosmist, the cosmos is a call to conquest. As we wrote in **Masters of the Will**:

> The cosmos calls to the greatest among us. Stranded here upon this backwater planet, with dreams of galactic conquest and limitless vistas to the stars, our memories of past imperial glories preserved within our holocrons, how can we be content with this puny, Earthbound existence? How can we be satisfied to conquer just one planet, when untold billions await?

A Sense of Urgency

Sith understand that the universe is at war with us and there is no time to be complacent. Our window of opportunity for getting off this planet and beginning construction of the Galactic Empire may be closing, never to open again. As British astronomer Fred Hoyle observed in 1964, this technological civilization offers only one shot for cosmic glory:

> It has often been said that, if the human species fails to make a go of it here on the Earth, some other species will take over the running. In the sense of

developing intelligence this is not correct. We have or soon will have, exhausted the necessary physical prerequisites so far as this planet is concerned. With coal gone, oil gone, high-grade metallic ores gone, no species however competent can make the long climb from primitive conditions to high-level technology. This is a one-shot affair. If we fail, this planetary system fails so far as intelligence is concerned.

With many non-renewable resources expected to run out during the next century, this civilization may have little time left to make good on its "one shot" of becoming spacefaring, and going on to conquer the galaxy and beyond.

The sociologist William Sims Bainbridge has recently made a related point, emphasizing the possible onset of stagnation and the urgent need for a new expansive spirit:

> At the moment it seems we have stopped leaping. We may be returning to the moon, and there could be some value in establishing a permanent base there. However the value of the International Space Station has been approximately nil, so we cannot count on great discoveries at the lunar south pole. The moon is being billed as a stepping stone to Mars, but any Martian expedition using technology currently under development would be far too modest to become the seed of a colony. To become fully interplanetary, let alone interstellar, our society would need another leap—and it needs that leap very soon before world culture ossifies into secure uniformity, or decays into absolute chaos. We need a new spaceflight social movement capable of giving a sense of transcendent purpose to dominant sectors of the society. It also should be capable of holding the society in an expansionist phase for the longest possible time, without permitting divergence from its great plan. In

short, we need a galactic religion, a Cosmic Order.

A galactic religion and a Cosmic Order; what could fit the bill better than Sith Cosmism and the Galactic Empire?

Since it is a cosmological certainty that our planet will be destroyed, if not by an asteroid impact then by the aging sun scorching our planet, we cannot afford to fail our one shot. The fate of earth-based life may hinge on what the next few generations choose to believe about the importance of space exploration. If this understanding were more common, wouldn't human beings be much more supportive of space programs, and more willing to embrace the Sith galactic agenda? Shouldn't Sith agents work to guide and promote space programs, by infiltrating them and recruiting key players into our Order? What if a few prominent space moguls, such as Elon Musk or Jeff Bezos, were secretly converted to Sithism, and began styling themselves after Darth Sidious or Darth Vader? Imagine what could be achieved if men with such resources and ambition were aligned with us!

It is worth noting in that regard that the American space program was heavily infiltrated from its earliest days by cults with their own agendas. There were three main factions: Freemasons, Nazis and Occultists. For example, there were Freemason astronauts John Glenn and Buzz Aldrin, ex-SS member and NASA head Wernher von Braun, and pioneering rocket engineer and Aleister Crowley disciple John Whiteside Parsons—all key figures in building America's space program into a moon-conquering powerhouse. The point is, there is a precedent for infiltration of space programs with occult agendas, and a reason they do so: because they understand the cosmic importance of space as we do, and the potential power to be gained. So we should follow their lead and either place our own people in these organizations or recruit existing personnel to the Dark Side and inspire them with visions of the Galactic Empire.

Religion for a Cosmic Civilization

Sith Cosmism is a philosophy of personal empowerment, but it is also a cosmic religion that can guide and inspire humanity toward the establishment of a vastly greater galactic civilization. During my pre-Sith days as a proponent of Cosmism, I (Darth Imperius) came across a visionary sociologist named William Sims Bainbridge who had studied religion and grasped the need for a cosmic religion at this moment in history. In an essay called *"Religion for a Galactic Civilization 2.0"* written in 2009, he described the current predicament of humanity, and called for a new religiosity to drive future space exploration. It is an inspiring read, and I have no disagreements with his conclusions. Modern civilization does indeed stand above an abyss, unable to return to the myopic old religions of the past and unlikely to move forward into a cosmic future without a new kind of religiosity. Here are two excerpts that summarize Bainbridge's compelling message:

> At the moment it seems we have stopped leaping. We may be returning to the moon, and there could be some value in establishing a permanent base there. However the value of the International Space Station has been approximately nil, so we cannot count on great discoveries at the lunar south pole. The moon is being billed as a stepping stone to Mars, but any Martian expedition using technology currently under development would be far too modest to become the seed of a colony. To become fully interplanetary, let alone interstellar, our society would need another leap—and it needs that leap very soon before world

culture ossifies into secure uniformity, or decays into absolute chaos. We need a new spaceflight social movement capable of giving a sense of transcendent purpose to dominant sectors of the society. It also should be capable of holding the society in an expansionist phase for the longest possible time, without permitting divergence from its great plan. In short, we need a galactic religion, a Cosmic Order. ...

The night is falling, and we do not have much time. We are all dying, and the cancer patient who has been told he has six months to live may be run over by a truck tomorrow. We give birth astride a grave, and a person's whole life is only a brief fall from nonexistence into oblivion. As the philosopher Nietzsche noted, we are balanced precariously on a tightrope across an abyss. We cannot go back, into the numbing faith of ancient superstitions, for science has destroyed the world in which they were plausible. We cannot stand here, because the winds of change are blowing and the resonating tightrope will sling our civilization into the chasm if it does not advance. So we must press forward, knowing that every perilous step might be our last.

But look! I see an eternal land beyond the far rim, where love thrives and death's sorrow never touches. Let us go there, you and I!

"Ossifying into secure conformity" is indeed a grave threat, as the totalitarian tentacles of tech-empowered corporations and governments wind ever tighter around the human mind, body and soul, while embracing an insipid slave moralism that aligns well with their control agenda. The other threat, of civilization "decaying into absolute chaos" also looms large on the horizon, as various environmental, cultural and economic trends hasten the collapse of civilization just as the system seems poised to assert global control.

In either case, Sith Cosmism offers an antidote. Against soulless techno-totalitarianism we offer an order that values Force power, individual greatness, moral freedom, metaphysical vision and revitalizing conflict over soul-crushing collectivism, meaningless materialism or enervating peace. Against degenerate anarchy we offer *the Empire*, an ordered, hierarchical civilization that offers anyone from any strata the opportunity to achieve greatness if they have the craving, the will and the Force power.

Note that in the Nietzsche quote referenced by Bainbridge above, Nietzsche's statement was *"Man is a rope stretched between the animal and the Superman—a rope over an abyss."* Thus Bainbridge is implying what Nietzsche prophesied, that humanity's path forward over the abyss of nihilism and stagnation would be to evolve physically, culturally and spiritually into Supermen. Nietzsche also said that "man needs what is most evil in him for what is best in him", implying that the path toward Superhumanity requires man to become more evil, and to jettison the moralism that keeps him chained to a doomed earth. This path of evolution, or *evilution*, of Man into Superman is central to our Sith project. And the Cosmos, which threatens to destroy us while it challenges us to achieve Galactic Empire and godhood, stands as the great bridge to the future, across which only a race of Supermen may stride. All of this is entailed in our vision of Sith Cosmism—a religion ambitious and evil enough for a cosmic civilization.

ACOSMISM

In contrast to Cosmism, which views the physical universe as the ultimate reality and stage for one's power plays, *Acosmism* is the school of thought that believes the material universe is an illusion or projection of the mind, and that beneath all appearances of substance there is nothing but emptiness or the Void. In other words, where Cosmism subsumes all gods and metaphysical constructs into the physical world, Acosmism subsumes all physical constructs into the metaphysical world.

Acosmism is prevalent in traditional mystical thought, particularly in the East. Indian Vedanta mystics call the manifest universe *Maya*—an illusion or deception that masks the ultimate, unmanifest reality called *Brahman*. Maya creates the illusion of *dualism*—the sense that the self is distinct from the external world. The goal of Vedantic practice is to liberate oneself from the illusion of Maya and realize one's unity with all things in a universal, "divine" consciousness. Buddhists incorporate similar Acosmist ideas with their doctrine of *Shunyata*. Shunyata is the belief that all phenomena are devoid of intrinsic nature; that beneath appearances generated by the mind, all things are formless aspects of the Void. The goal of Buddhist meditation is to become aware of the illusory nature of all forms and realize the deeper reality of Shunyata—including the realization that one's self is an illusion.

Other varieties of Acosmism posit that the ultimate reality is God, and the material world is a trap or illusion designed to test the faith of human beings in preparation for their real, eternal life in the hereafter. This form of Acosmism is found in mystical Christian, Islamic and Gnostic sects. Even some modern scientific materialists have expressed an Acosmist sensibility, by suggesting that the world we take for reality might actually be a computer simulation—a virtual reality, created by a material substrate that seeks to make existence more interesting. But ultimately, even if we exist in a simulation of a simulation, ad infinitum, the underlying substrate is very simple, and rather boring. This is essentially a restatement of Vedantic Acosmism in modern technological terms.

Now we ask: what is Dark Acosmism, and what value could it have to a Sith? How can rejecting the phenomenal world as illusory contribute to one's power? The short answer is that Acosmism, like all things, has a Dark Side that can be a powerful tool of metaphysical liberation.

Recall that in our discussion of Black Sunnite metaphysics we spoke of the *White Sunlit-World* and the *Shadow World*, which play similar roles as Maya and Brahman in Vedanta. This is a Dark Acosmist doctrine, which embraces formlessness *(chanbrânûk)* as the primal reality and rejects the formed world *(chanagum-thûl)* as an ephemeral emanation from the Void. Only the eternal Shadow World of the *Dâr* is real; the White Sun-lit world of forms is illusory and fleeting. The Dark Acosmist is not interested in any science or sensual activity that only serves to further entangle him in the illusory web of material forms. What interests the Dark Acosmist are those arts and sciences that can cut through the White Sun-lit web of illusions: metaphysical reflections, Void meditations and magickal incantations that dispel the "curse" of matter and clear the mind to perceive the Shadow World behind all forms.

A simple example of such an Acosmist incantation was given in Book Two of this series, **Masters of the Will**, in the form of the *Fetter-Cutting Code*:

By my Sword of Will I cut this fetter from me;
By my Sword of Will I set my spirit free.

This simple spell may be used when faced with any material obstacle, to willfully reject its power over your spirit, thus cutting one more strand of the illusory web that fetters you to the things of this world.

A fully realized Dark Acosmist might resemble a sinister Lama or Zen master in his advanced metaphysical understanding and lack of attachment to the things of the formed world. An Acosmist mystic can meditate serenely as people die, civilizations erode and empires crumble to dust; an Acosmist black magician can feel no remorse as he ritually transfers the souls of his enemies into mustard seeds and grinds them between millstones while chanting mantras to his demon-gods, in the manner of the Tibetan lama-sorcerers. The inhuman or reptilian levels of detachment that may be attained by an Acosmist Dark Lord can be quite disturbing to the uninitiated, and make him in some ways the most fearsome and rarefied type of Dark Lord. To possess a passion, not for the material conquest or destruction of the world, but for the rejection of its very reality, is not a path many beings would wish to tread, but for those few "Dark Buddhas" who walk it, it can be a most liberating and powerful path indeed.

Of course, the Sith Acolyte may always choose to refute Acosmism in the manner of Conan the Barbarian, who said:

"Let teachers and priests and philosophers brood over questions of reality and illusion. I know this: if life is illusion, then I am no less an illusion, and being thus, the illusion is real to me. I live, I burn with life, I love, I slay, and am content."

Anti-Cosmism

Anti-Cosmism is the inverse of Cosmism: where Cosmists embrace the universe as a means to glorification and godhood, the Anti-Cosmist rejects the universe entirely and believes that it should not even exist. The Anti-Cosmist is in spiritual opposition not only to the material universe, but to whatever god or force said "let there be Light" and brought it into existence.

To illustrate Anti-Cosmism, we will describe two sects: one imagined into existence by Darth Imperius, and one created for the Star Wars literary universe. There are other examples we could discuss, such as the *Temple of the Black Light*—a Swedish order with a complex cosmology called "Chaosophy", one of whose members ritually murdered another then committed suicide. Obviously, Anti-Cosmism is a path fraught with danger and is not for the spiritually timid or those who find anything in this world sacred—including their own lives.

Black Sunnism

Black Sunnites are beings "born under the wrong sun", who feel like they've been exiled here from a Black Sun-lit world for a special mission. For their kind, anything that undermines the creator gods and their creation is doing sacred work to dispel the White Sun illusions, unblind the eyes of the White Sunnite slaves, and manifest the deeper truths of the Black Sun-dominated universe. The Black Sunnite practices Black Alchemy (*Borashmârkâr):* a process of reorienting oneself mentally and spiritually so that the seemingly dispiriting, demoralizing reality of our *Borzûmik* universe becomes a source of passion and inspiration. The Black Sunnite learns to find glory in death, beauty in destruction and joy in the Void. Thus do they convert darkness into passion and Force power, becoming holy warriors on a path of destruction, seeking ever more Force power from the Shadow-Sun to empower their great work.

Black Sunnites have made Anti-Cosmism the foundation of their cult's philosophy. They subscribe to a creed called the *Nine Terrible Truths*, three of which are: "the world is dying", "the gods are hostile", and "Darkness is our destiny." Black Sunnism is thus an ideal path for the Acolyte who feels at war with all reality, and seeks not to conquer it so much as destroy it. We encourage Sith Acolytes to study Black Sunnism as a way to explore the furthest extremes of Dark Side thought and to develop their own *Black Diamond minds*. To learn more about this darkest of Dark Side philosophies, look for our future publication, **Book of the Black Sun**.

The Way of the Dark

In the Star Wars Extended Universe, there is a sect called the *Sorcerers of Rhand* who follow an extreme Anti-Cosmist path called the *Way of the Dark*. Below is an excerpt from the novel *"Luke Skywalker and the Shadows of Mindor,"* by Matthew Stover, in which this powerful group and their fascinating philosophy was first introduced.

> The Sorcerers of Rhand ... had forged him as a weapon is forged, awakening his insight, refining his will, opening his mind to the One Truth:
>
> Only power is real, and the only real power is the power to destroy. Existence is fleeting. Destruction is eternal.
>
> Every child was born waiting for death. Civilizations fell, and their very ashes were swallowed by time. The stars themselves burned out. Destruction, on the other hand...

Destruction was the will of the universe.

Some called it entropy, and tried to quantify and constrain it with the laws of thermodynamics. Some expressed it with a simple poetic declarative: Things fall apart. Some even tried to dismiss it with a joke: Anything that can go wrong will. But it was not a joke, or poetry; it was not science, nor was it subject to any law.

It was the Way of the Dark.

Destruction was easy... and permanent. When a being was killed, everything he or she would have ever done or possessed, seen or felt, was murdered. And that murder made a *permanent change in the structure of the universe*—it emptied the universe of an entire life, and left behind only a void.

That void was the foundation of truth.

That was why the Jedi and the Sith would remain forever locked in their pointless battle: because all their philosophy of light versus dark, of service versus mastery, was as meaningless as the whistle of wind through desert rocks. Service and mastery were equally futile, even illusory, in the face of the One Truth. All the endless Jedi vs. Sith nattering of "the dark side of the Force" blinded them one and all to the bare reality that there was nothing *but* the Dark.

The Black Sun Jihad

{ Even an ideology as extreme and destructive as Anti-Cosmism could potentially become the basis of a great Empire. The following little story illustrates how an Anti-Cosmist civilization might arise that, like the Sorcerers of Rhand, seeks greatness through universal destruction. }

Untold millions of years ago, a civilization in another galaxy went through a period of intellectual "Enlightenment" much like our own, in which science and rationality triumphed over ancient traditions of religiosity and mysticism. But soon after this came the "Endarkenment", a period of cultural disillusionment characterized by cosmicist artists, nihilist philosophers and mystics of the Void. For them, the universe revealed by science turned out to be too strange, indifferent and doomed to be reconciled with notions of progress or cosmic benevolence. Thus was born the *Black Sunnite* movement: a quasi-religious cult founded by endarkened intellectuals who looked at reality unsentimentally and concluded that life, consciousness and the universe itself were abominations that should not even exist.

Soon after this revelation the Black Sunnites launched the *Black Sun Jihad*—the holy war to eradicate all life in the cosmos, by launching self-replicating planet-killing machines into space in all directions. The machines constructed a kind of *Dyson sphere*, or shell, around each star, blotting out its light long enough to freeze the solar system to death. In this way, the Black Sun Armada sterilized their entire home galaxy of life long ago, and are approaching ours as we speak. Any day now, perhaps, their doomsday machines will arrive, and soon after our sun will go black, and our planet will die, forever.

Cosmicism

The fourth cosmic school of thought, *Cosmicism*, takes its name from the literarary philosophy conceived by the visionary writer Howard Phillips Lovecraft. Cosmicism posits that human concerns are of no significance in the larger cosmic scheme of things; that the universe is an incomprehensibly vast, alien and indifferent void, upon which we project our values in a futile attempt to console ourselves in the face of our puniness. Lovecraft described this worldview rather poetically in this passage:

> The human race will disappear. Other races will appear and disappear in turn. The sky will become icy and void, pierced by the feeble light of half-dead stars. Which will also disappear. Everything will disappear. And what human beings do is just as free of sense as the free motion of elementary particles. Good, evil, morality, feelings? Pure 'Victorian fictions'. Only egotism exists.

Note that Cosmicism is not nihilism; it allows for the possibility of ego-created values and purpose, but it simply denies that they are universally meaningful. To some god-like extraterrestrial beings we might encounter in the Cosmos, like the amorphous Azathoth and Nyarlothotep of Lovecraft's tales, our values would be as meaningless as the values of microbes are to us. Our ancestral religions in particular, with their Earth- and human-centered mythologies which claim to possess universal values, are obviously absurd and delusional from a Cosmicist perspective.

But more disturbingly from a Cosmist point of view, Cosmicism not only refutes the pretensions of religion, but takes a deeply pessimistic view of the scientific enterprise as well—as expressed in the famous opening paragraph of Lovecraft's story "The Call of Cthulhu":

> The most merciful thing in the world, I think, is the inability of the human mind to correlate all its contents. We live on a placid island of ignorance in the midst of black seas of infinity, and it was not meant that we should voyage far. The sciences, each

> straining in its own direction, have hitherto harmed us little; but some day the piecing together of dissociated knowledge will open up such terrifying vistas of reality, and of our frightful position therein, that we shall either go mad from the revelation or flee from the light into the peace and safety of a new dark age.

Here we have a philosophical proposition to horrify the scientific rationalist: that the entire Enlightenment project, by which the light of reason illuminates the dark corners of human ignorance and thereby improves the human condition, is little more than a dangerous delusion; that in fact science has opened a Pandora's Box which will destroy us all. Yet what thinking being, whether inclined toward the Dark Side or the Light, can dismiss Lovecraft's contention? Doesn't recent history suggest that we, in our relentless quest for knowledge, venturing ever further from our placid island of ignorance, risk unleashing horrors which threaten us with an all-encompassing doom? Doesn't the "Great Silence" of a universe with no signs of extraterrestrial intelligence suggest that scientific knowledge may lead inexorably to self-destruction?

Lovecraft died before the horrors of World War Two, the dawn of the nuclear age, SETI, Chernobyl, the Large Hadron Collider, Comet Shoemaker-Levy, 9/11, Global Warming or the advent of deep sea oil drilling that threatens entire ecosystems with destruction. Nor could even his fertile imagination have foreseen such looming 21st century abominations as genetic engineering, nanotechnology and robotics run amok. But it's doubtful that any of these monstrous spawn of the rationalist scientific project would have surprised him. Are they not further proof that we are living in a Lovecraftian age of existential terror, in which

Lovecraft's philosophy of cosmic pessimism becomes ever more compelling?

Cosmicism is indeed a powerful thought-bomb; those who encounter it for the first time may find themselves gripped by the horror of our cosmic predicament and become extreme pessimists or nihilists. Consider for a moment some of the bleak truths revealed by science: our sun is numerically less than one grain of sand among all the beaches of the Earth in comparison to the stars in the Cosmos; our universe is the stage for astrophysical annihilation on an unimaginably vast scale; the human species will eventually go extinct like any other, our biosphere will perish, our sun will burn out, our galaxy will collide with another or be swallowed by a supermassive black hole, the universe will end in heat death, and there are no gods appearing to save any of it. Our consciousness and all our creations are doomed by entropy to perish before long. Surely Lovecraft must have been right: human life is utterly absurd, insignificant and without higher purpose. We can pursue egotistical projects or worship various gods, but ultimately it is a futile exercise. As Clark Ashton Smith, Lovecraft's gifted literary colleague, put it:

> "All human thought, all science, all religion, is the holding of a candle to the night of the universe."

Sith who embrace Cosmicism will tend toward pessimism and nihilism. But rather than seeking to destroy the universe like the Anti-Cosmicists, they will look to magickal and artistic creation as their source of power, and "laugh off" the universe as a bad joke. Or they might embrace some kind of Cosmicist cultism, such as the "Cthulhu cults" of Lovecraft's stories, which seek some kind of transcendent, religious gnosis in the bleak cosmic truth. The Dark Lords have conceived one such cult themselves, the *Cult of Xoth*, dedicated to the Lovecraftian "Outer Gods"—for more information, see their book *Black Templar Handbook*.

It is up to each Acolyte of the Sith Path to determine which of the above four cosmic schools of thought they subscribe to. Traditionally, the Sith tend toward Cosmism, as it is a natural fit for our ideology of Galactic imperialism, but all four are viable Dark Side cosmic philosophies of empowerment and empire. We leave it as Challenge #8 of this Echelon for you to determine which is best for you.

ASPECTS OF SITHISM

In this chapter we discuss various aspects of Sithism, as a philosophy, religion and way of life that is distinct from all other paths.

THE SITH CODE

The *Sith Code* was a mantra that encapsulated the philosophy of the legendary Sith of the Galaxy Far, Far Away. Darth Bane, founder of the Rule of Two, credits this code with transforming him into a Sith Lord:

> *Peace is a lie. There is only passion.*
> *Through passion I gain strength.*
> *Through strength I gain power.*
> *Through power I gain victory.*
> *Through victory my chains are broken.*
> *The Force shall free me.*

While this Code is not Sith Academy's Code, nor a creation of the Dark Lords, it is a powerful statement of Sith philosophy that is worth analyzing in more detail.

"Peace is a lie; there is only passion."

This expresses the empirical fact that peace does not exist, except as a religious fantasy or unattainable ideal. This world is an arena of eternal conflict; to be alive is to be in a state of war—with nature, other beings and yourself. In our tongue we call this a *Shâz-Vrâthûl (War Universe)*. To preach peace is to preach a lie—useful perhaps to pacify enemies you wish to conquer, but not to fool yourself!

The second part of this stanza makes an even stronger claim: that in a War Universe, passion is all you have. This makes sense, because the moment you lose your passion for life and no longer wish to fight for anything is the moment you begin to die. This universe requires passion for existence; perhaps there are more peaceful universes where passion is not required for survival, but that is not the one we inhabit. And the passion that compels us to win the struggle for life is precisely what we call *the Force*, or *Zy*.

But what of dispassionate reason, the trait so beloved of Light Side philosophers? That is secondary; one can rationalize anything, including one's own non-existence. There have been untold numbers of rational people who gave up and died because they lacked passion, but seldom does a passionate person give up. Reason must be the slave of passion, as the saying goes, because survival in this War Universe requires it to be so!

"Through passion I gain strength."

This stanza follows from what has already been said. Passion brings a reason to engage fully in the struggle for life, which strengthens a being physically, psychically, and spiritually. Passion is Force, which brings vitality, strength of will and single-mindedness of purpose. It wells up from the unconscious mind, which is the seat of your power as a Sith, guides your conscious mind and infuses you whole being with energy. Other things being equal, a being with greater passion for the struggle, rooted in an unconscious Source, will prevail over beings who lack such passion.

"Through strength I gain power."

The accumulation of inner strength and vitality gives one an infectious energy and a dominating presence that others will naturally find compelling. You will find that the whole world seems to bend magically to your will and unconscious mind. This ability to compel others and shape your reality brings power, for that is what power is.

"Through power I gain victory."

The ability to compel others brings victories, for obvious reasons. A general of an army conquers when he has the allegiance of his men; an athlete becomes a champion when his body has been brought to its peak of power; a politician defeats his enemies when he wields dominating power over the minds of other men and thus defeats them, often without need for violence; a species prevails in the struggle for life when it dominates its environment. For the purpose of power in a War Universe is indeed to gain victory.

Through victory my chains are broken.

Victory means to vanquish enemies who threaten your power; to defeat those who kept you in chains or in some way limited your freedom of will and action. These enemies might be other individuals, nations, social systems, ideas, or forces of nature. By defeating them through struggle, you not only break the grip of their control mechanism, but you send a message to them and to yourself that you are no longer subject their their wills, and thus win a battle in the most important war of all: the war against self-limitation.

The Force shall free me.

As explained in *Lords of the Force*, the Force is the energy, passion and belief one acquires from a *Source* that infuses one's being with a sense of purpose and power. Possessing Force power means have a connection to a Source; having a Source connection means being freed from the chains of cultural conditioning and hostile Source systems, such as governments, laws, religions, narratives and social conventions. A being with such Force power is freed of all arbitrary man-made constructs, laws and philosophies; he need only follow the dictates of his Source to begin building his empire anew, no matter where in this War Universe he may find himself. This is what it means to find true freedom in the Force as a Dark Lord of the Sith.

Aspects of Sithism
The Scope of Sithism

Sithism is not intended as a philosophy for all of humanity, or for an entire class of people, but for a few select individuals who feel intuitively drawn to these ideas. The common mass of people, led by their sheep-herding intellectuals and priesthoods, will always scorn and vilify our kind, calling us a variety of names, such as "sociopaths", "psychopaths", "terrorists", "evil-doers", "fascists", "Satanists", etc. They have developed entire paradigms of thought, customs and laws to prevent our kind from having significant influence over the minds of their flock or wielding power over their societies.

It is not for such "mundane" or "Light Side" beings that we write, nor to whom we appeal for our Acolytes. We appeal to the exceptional, the unusual, the ingenious and the non-mundane—those who, for whatever reason, find the basic assumptions of Light Side philosophy dubious, ridiculous or repugnant. Sithism does not claim to have discovered the "objective truth", to have the solutions to the world's problems, to be humanity's "salvation", to be a means of "improving the world" or "liberating mankind". The value of Sithism lies within the minds and lives of select individuals, who will pursue it as a path to personal liberation, empowerment, expression, greatness and meaning. Sithism could be compared to an artistic or spiritual lineage more than a philosophical one; those who take up the black robes of our Order are expected to use their minds as weapons and tools of art, with which they paint awesome and terrible works upon the pages of history. A Sith philosopher of ten thousand years hence may be no closer to "the truth" than one of today, but he should be motivated by the same drive to greatness that drove our mythological forebears and which drives us to this day.

Sithism as Religion

Sithism as we conceive it is not just a philosophy, but a religion. It is rooted in an irrational faith in something called the Source, and the Force. Our Source, which has been called many names—the Dark Side, the Devil, the Dark Tao, the Black Sun—is for us a kind of god. It is the "dark Logos" or "Lucifer Principle" that drives the universe along on its path of destruction, and each being individually on his path of power.

Some Sith will be highly religious, even fanatical in their faith. For them, the Dark Side is an overwhelming presence in their lives, which they pay tribute to with frequent rituals and offerings, and whose will they seek to know by meditations and divinations. They will gravitate toward the Templar specialization, building Black Temples where they can invoke the Dark Force and lead religious rites in its honor. For other Sith, the Dark Side is a more abstract presence, which they intuit or reason about philosophically with minimal religious and occult trappings.

What distinguishes the Dark Side religion from its Light Side counterparts is its emphasis on individual empowerment and attainment of godhood, rather than submission to the power of a religious institution, prophet, holy book or god.

The Dark Side does not demand submission and mindless obedience, but it does reward those who advance its power in the world. Sith religion resembles dark paganism or deistic Satanism, in which rituals and offerings are made to the dark Force as a kind of power trade, much as a Devil-worshipper makes pacts with Satan. For the Sith do worship the Dark Side, make offerings to it, seek to know and do its will, and in turn invoke Dark Side power for personal gain.

An Occult Path

Sithism is an *occult* path of knowledge. This means we do not seek to make all our knowledge of the Dark Side widely known, because that is both impossible and undesirable. *Impossible*, because much of the knowledge we speak of cannot be understood by ordinary individuals, who have not undergone an initiatory process to change their consciousness and transform their being into vessels of power and not mere intellectual exponents of a philosophy. *Undesirable*, because knowledge of the secrets of power is itself power, and in a universe ruled by evilution, it is rather foolish to hand others keys to power which may then be used against you. So we Sith must be secretive and selective in disseminating our knowledge of the Dark Side. What we reveal in our books is like a beacon lit up to attract the right sorts of beings, who flutter toward it like dark moths to a black flame. But the full meaning of our teachings will only be understood via personal gnosis under the guidance of an endarkened Master.

Sith philosophy is also occult in that we do not attempt to argue by reason for that which we do know. We do not follow modern rationalist methodology, because the power of the Force lies beyond the gates of reason and the citadels of science. We do not attempt to explain the Dark Side according to the methods of philosophy or science, so much as to be consumed by its mystery and charged with its power. Thus Sithism is not a philosophy in the Western, Greek rationalist sense, but a path of gnosis, inspiration and empowerment, more akin to the ways sorcerers, shamans and mystics understood the world long before philosophy came on the scene.

A Path of Inversion

> "Light will for a time have to be called darkness: this is the path you must tread." —Friedrich Nietzsche

The path of the Dark Side is a path of inversion; it requires you to learn to call many "evil" things "good", and many "good" things "evil". Light for a Darksider will be called Darkness by the Lightsiders, and Darkness is what they call our Light. To go down this Path means entering a portal into a mirror inner universe, where the Black Sun dominates the sky rather than the White Sun, and the moral concepts of the Light Side creeds are turned on their heads. But those who are destined for this Path should already know this; they should feel, deep in their Shadow-minds from a young age, that they are different from other beings; that their spiritual polarity is "flipped". Discovering the Dark Path should feel like finding one's natural spiritual home and awakening to one's destiny.

Sith are a Force-Race

The Sith are a "race of the spirit", or a *Zy-zhâr*, which means "Force-tribe" in our Black Tongue. This means we transmit our endarkened minds and spirits across generations so as to preserve a certain breed of being—not via genetic replication, but by Force transmission from Masters to Apprentices.

Here "Force transmission" *(Zy-mashât)* refers to the process of imprinting a Dark Lord's *Force-essence*—his belief in a Source, his techniques for channelling the Source's Force power, his language, lore and personality—onto his Apprentices. The Master brings the Apprentice into connection with the Sith *egregore:* the collective "Force-being" created and maintained by the thoughts and wills of Sith Masters and Apprentices down through the ages. This connection overrides any genetic or cultural programming the Apprentice may bring with him, imprinting upon him a new identity as a Sith that defines him and instills in him a desire to propagate it to his own descendants. This Force transmission is an intense, initiatory process that can only take place under direct, prolonged tutelage by a Sith Master. The process is very difficult, and few will complete it. Thus do we ensure that the Sith remain a highly selective Force-race, never large in number, but always of the highest quality and power!

The Sith Force Order

In Sith society, indviduals acquire authority not according to their wealth, heredity, educational credentials, military might or rank within some secular political hierarchy, but according to their *Zy-Raka*—Force power. We establish a *Force Order (Zy-Gâzûl)* to rank beings according to their mastery of the Dark Side of the Force. To do this, we have established a series of ranks within the Order, from highest to lowest in Force power:

1) **The Ruling Two:** The two supreme Dark Lords who lead the Sith Order.

2) **Dark Lords:** Individuals who have completed their Nine Echelons training and been personally initiated into Dark Lordship by the Ruling Two.

3) **Apprentices:** Individuals who have advanced far

enough in their training that a Dark Lord has taken a personal interest in their development.

4) **Acolytes:** Individuals who have begun their Nine Echelons training via the Dark Lords' books and/or interaction with other Sith.

5) **Black Agents:** Individuals who are attracted to the Dark Lords' vision and support it in some way, but haven't become Initiates of the Order.

Power and authority flows from the Sith Order's Source—the Dark Side—down through the ranks of the Order. Everyone outside the Order, or an allied Force Order, is considered a "Lightsider" or a "mundane"—a Forceless being of no power or importance, until proven otherwise.

SITH SPIRITUALITY

Rejection of Slave Moralism

The Dark Lords perceive a profound sickness at the core of the Abrahamic Source System, originating in Judaism and metastasizing in Christianity. This sickness, apparent to many ancient peoples who first encountered these religions, was the pathology of the poor, the weak and the wretched, who by an audacious act of black magick, asserted their moral superiority over the strong, noble, aristocratic rulers of the classical age. The philosopher Nietzsche was the first influential thinker of modern times to give the core sickness of Abrahamic religion a name: *slave morality*—which he describes thus:

> "Of all that has been done on earth against "the noble", "the mighty", "the lords", "the power-holders", nothing is worthy of mention in comparison with that which the *Jews* have done against them: the Jews,

> that priestly people who in the end were only able to obtain satisfaction from their enemies and conquerors through a radical revaluation of their values, that is, through an act of spiritual revenge... It was the Jews who in opposition to the aristocratic value equation (good = noble = powerful = beautiful = happy = beloved of God) dared its inversion, with fear-inspiring consistency, and it held it with the teeth of the most unfathomable hate (the hate of powerlessness), namely: 'the miserable alone are the good; the poor, powerless, lowly alone are the good; the suffering, deprived, sick, ugly are also the only pious, the only blessed in God, for them alone is there blessedness – whereas you, you noble and powerful ones, you are in all eternity the evil, the cruel, the lustful, the insatiable, the godless, you will eternally be the wretched, accursed, the damned!'"

Nietzsche goes on to describe how this slave moralism spread across the classical world via Christianity, completely overturning its values and toppling its regimes. So successful has this campaign of Abrahamic black magick been that slave moralism continues to dominate the values of Western civilization even now, long after the death-grip of Christianity upon its thought-leaders has been broken. For modern "secular progressives" have internalized most of the same slave moralism, and continue to preach against the evils of privilege and power in a spirit that ancient Jews and Christians would have no trouble understanding.

The Third and Fourth Spiritual Poles

It has been said that Western thought has two poles around which it revolves, or two capitols from which it flows: ancient Athens and Jerusalem.

Athens represents the pole of Reason; the place where

Western philosophy originated, mathematics and science flowered, and rationalism attained its greatest heights in the ancient world. For 2500 years, Western thought has owed much to the ancient Greeks—to the likes of Socrates, Plato, Aristotle and Archimedes, who created so many of the thoughtforms that still guide Western civilization. To some this is the only pole that is needed; rational philosophy, such people say, can totally replace irrational faith and tradition as the individual and collective source of meaning.

Jerusalem represents the pole of Faith; the place where the Jewish temples stood, Jesus was crucified, and Christians and Jews locate their spiritual centers. With the Christian conversion of Rome, the subsequent Christianization of Europe and its expansion across the globe, Jerusalem became the spiritual capitol of the Westernized world, and the place from which it derives its highest moral guidance. To many, a modern civilization that disregards Jerusalem is a soulless, pagan order, if not the Antichrist System itself.

For the Dark Lords, this bipolar spiritual alignment within one civilization is pathological and unsatisfactory, just as a bipolar personality is pathological and unsatisfactory for a human mind. Not only do the two poles directly conflict on many issues, but they omit vast areas of human thought and experience that are neither comprehensible to Greek rationalism nor acceptable to Judean moralism. To us, these two poles act like hostile spells that starve the souls of men, leaving them hungry for another order that can satisfy the cravings of their shadow-minds. We have identified two other spiritual poles that may satisfy these cravings, which we call the pole of *Rome* and the pole of *the Wild*.

The pole of Rome represents the *Imperium*: the vast empire that expresses man's longing for power, pageantry and greatness on a grand scale. When one aligns spiritually with

Rome, one seeks to be part of something greater than oneself; to march under the banner of a great emperor, to conquer others and glorify oneself in the process. Every great imperialist has felt this longing powerfully, and every lasting empire has nurtured it. But this pole often conflicts with the poles of Athens and Jerusalem, which counsel values such as democracy, liberty and equality that are at odds with the imperatives of imperium—a conflict that explains why Western civilization has found itself in so many wars with foreign empires. It also explains why this civilization plays the empire game so poorly, and seems unlikely to keep winning unless it rediscovers the pole of Rome and truly believes in it.

The fourth pole, *the Wild*, represents the wild pagan spirit of the forests, mountains and deserts, and the primal darkness of the night and the Void. The unknown, the evil, the uncivilized, the doomed, the terrifying—these are anathema not only to both poles of Western thought, but to Rome and its campaign to crush barbarians and push back the wilderness.

What we are proposing with our Sith Empire project is to overthrow the bipolar tyranny of Athens and Jerusalem, and to erect a new Empire animated by the spirit of both Rome and the Wild. This will establish a new "Wild Imperium" pole, which we locate geographically at the site of our Black Temple, but which exists in every place, time and soul that remains wild and unbroken by the slave religions and sterile philosophies that created them.

The Power of Transgression

Any barrier erected against powerful thought or behavior creates a build-up of energy, much like a dam creates water pressure or a wall around a nation creates political pressure.

Aspects of Sithism

The breaking of that barrier—by transgressing whatever law, moral code, military force or social convention put it in place—therefore causes a release of energy. This release of energy can become an explosion—a cultural or political revolution, military conquest or spiritual revelation. This energy released by transgression can then be harnessed by the Sith black magician on his path of power.

What kind of energy are we talking about here? As we see it, all energy released by transgression, whether it manifests in the cultural, political, spiritual or personal domains, is of one metaphysical type: the energy we call *the Force*. To understand this, remember that the Force is passion and belief; it is the inner fire that motivates men to struggle, build and conquer, to overcome all obstacles to their acquisition of power. Whenever a limitation is placed upon one's ability to cultivate power, in the form of laws, customs or limiting beliefs, those who receive a constant flow of Force from a Source will experience a build-up of "Force pressure" that has nowhere to go. They find their will to power blocked by external barriers, or barriers created by their own minds, and must await a transgressive event that breaks down these barriers and liberates their pent-up Force energy.

This process of transgression and release of energy is the key to black magick. In the old grimoires, the sorcerer is instructed to carry out a series of difficult, bizarre and gruesome acts, such as stealing bones from a coffin, drinking blood, engaging in sexual perversions or sacrificing animals. Whatever metaphysical effects such rites may have upon the larger cosmos, they will surely change one's inner cosmos, by breaking through various personal taboos that have limited one's sense of possibility. This will be experienced as a sense of revulsion, but also as exhilaration.

One's old limiting beliefs will be broken, allowing one to enter a larger mental and spiritual world.

The power of transgression doesn't have to involve acts that are gruesome or morally repugnant; one can break boundaries and release energy by doing something that has never been done before and was previously thought to be impossible, such as flying an airplane, swimming the English Channel, climbing Mount Everest or walking on the moon. Such acts are also transgressive of Force barriers and act as a type of black magick. So is joining a Dark Side Order, creating a cult, conquering a nation or building an empire. All such transgressive activities can and should be pursued by Sith disciples, not simply in pursuit of mundane power, fame or shock value, but to release unlimited Force energies which we can harness on our paths of unlimited power.

Primalism

As we have already stated, Sithism is an anti-philosophy; it is not intended as another convoluted system of rationalist abstractions and laws, such as have plagued humanity since the onset of civilizations and slave religions, but a return to a more primal state of being before philosophy, religion and civilization came on the scene. We embrace the ethos of the pre-civilized men and uncivilized beasts, who live in a state of instinctive intelligence, power-craving, flow in the moment and full awareness of the dark and sinister nature of this world. Sithism is intended as a cure for hyper-rationalism, the cowardice of the intellectuals, the disenchantment of the world, the moralist delusions of the priests, and other pathologies that Light Side philosophy has wrought. We call this aspect of our anti-philosophy *primalism,* which means a return to first principles, first states of consciousness and first motives. We practice it on our path via meditation, magick rituals, nature immersion, embrace of conflict, psychedelics, seduction, art, athletics, and other techniques for defeating the "inner philosopher" who distracts us from our primal nature and power. Primalism represents an end to philosophy and a return to a pre-philosophical state of being—a development which the most insightful philosophers, such as Nietzsche, Heidegger, Taoists, Chaoists and Zen Buddhists, have all pointed to as the way out of the cul-de-sac of philosophy.

Actionism

Sithism is also path of action; even the most philosophical Sith prefers actions to words, real-life tests to thought experiments, heroic deeds to grandiose thoughts. He leaves impotent philosophizing to the coffeeshop warriors and mountaintop mystics, preferring to go out onto the streets and into the corridors of power to test his ideas and seek his destiny. The proof of a Sith's philosophy is not found in his clever arguments or moralistic appeals, but in his real-world victories and successes. As Darth Imperius put it:

> The true test of our philosophy is war; the real measure of our Force mastery is power; the highest truth of Sithism is victory.

In philosophical terms, this is a form of *empiricism*—the notion that evidence and results determine which ideas are true, rather their "innate truth". But we prefer to call it *actionism (âtodûn)*, emphasizing the inherent value of action, of engaging in the struggle for power, even though one might be defeated. The power that is gained via this struggle is not evidenced only by one's conquests on the physical plane, but by the inner, spiritual benefits—the Force power one gains by taking bold action.

Actionism aligns well with the "just do it" ethos of the modern Western world, as well as with Eastern warrior philosophies such as Zen Buddhism and Bushido. Bruce Lee was a favorite exponent of actionist philosophy, as evidenced in quotes like these:

> "If you spend too much time thinking about a thing, you'll never get it done. Make at least one definite move daily toward your goal."
>
> "Use only that which works, and take it from any place you can find it."
>
> "Defeat is a state of mind. No one is ever defeated until defeat has been accepted as reality. To me, defeat in anything is merely temporary, and its punishment is but an urge for me to greater effort to achieve my goal. Defeat simply tells me that something is wrong in my doing; it is a path leading to success and truth."

Also note that focused thought directed toward a goal is a type of action. The Sith philosopher or sorcerer who uses thought as a weapon is no less a warrior than the one who wields a sword. Putting ideas to the test, asserting them into the world and waging war on enemy ideologies can bring as much empowerment as physical actionism. This understanding is the essence of "Mind Power"—one of the Pillars of Sithism discussed in the next chapter.

THE NINE PILLARS OF SITHISM

Now we come to the heart of this book: the identification of the central tenets of Sithism. In the box below we list the nine *Pillars*, or fundamental precepts, of this path. Note that these Pillars do not constitute the entirety of Sithism, but are the nine most important concepts that set it apart from other paths and form the philosophical foundation of our Order.

> **The Nine Pillars of Sithism:**
>
> 1. The Primacy of Power
> 2. The Tao of Darwin
> 3. The Force and the Source
> 4. The Power of the Dark Side
> 5. The Superman
> 6. Mind Power
> 7. Multiversalism
> 8. Galactic Empire
> 9. Formlessness

Now let us discuss each Pillar in more detail.

The Primacy of Power

{ Pillar One was discussed extensively in Book One of this series: "The Path of Power"; we refer the reader there for further discussion. }

> "What is good? All that heightens the feeling of power, the Will to Power, power itself in man. What is bad? All that proceeds from weakness. What is happiness? The feeling that power *increases*—that a resistance is overcome." —Friedrich Nietzsche

The above quote summarizes the first Pillar of Sithism, sometimes called the *Diamond Rule (Gâmâzh-Kûm)*: that which makes you more powerful is good; that which weakens you is bad; that which gives you a feeling of empowerment is happiness.

We borrow the words of the dark side prophet Nietzsche for this Pillar, but it is an ancient principle, understood by all strong peoples before the coming of the slave moralists and Light Side orders. For all successful beings know without need of philosophy that more power is good, for only it can bring glory and ensure survival in a hostile world. No strong, free people ever adopted the ethos of the Light Side tribes, who preach that turning the other cheek and celebrating the weak is a path to salvation in the next world. In reality, only enslavement, defeat and death await those who violate the Diamond Rule, and the graveyards of history are littered with their bones.

So we advise the Acolyte to always remember Gâmâzh-Kûm and make it the first principle of your Sith Path of destiny. No matter what may confront you, simply ask: does this make me more powerful? If the answer is no, shun it, fight it, destroy it; if the answer is yes, seize it, embrace it, enhance it. Follow this simple rule, and you will find your body, mind and spirit becoming as hard as diamond, such that nothing can break or scratch them. You will also find yourself gaining victories over those who deny its truth; for just as diamond is much harder than gold, so are the disciples of the Diamond Rule much harder than disciples of the Golden Rule. If you have no other philosophy, remember this one rule and it alone may guide you to the heights of Sith greatness!

The Tao of Darwin

Darwinian evolution is the central fact of life on this planet. From the simplest microbes to the most complex intelligent life forms, from genes to memes, nations to corporations, everything in nature exists in a perpetual struggle for dominance. This struggle is the source of all progress, all empowerment, all evolution. The Sith therefore embrace Darwinism as a moral imperative.

Social Darwinism

The Sith subscribe to a "might is right", "survival of the fittest" ethos. We believe that only in the crucible of struggle, in which failure, weakness and apathy are punished and victory, strength and ambition are rewarded, can man achieve greatness and evolve into something still greater. We consider this a natural law, which every creature who has successfully engaged in the billion-year long struggle for life on this planet must obey. In the realm of human social and political systems, this natural law expresses itself as "Social Darwinism": a regime where the poor, unintelligent, unfit and unskilled are seen as burdens on society, who should be allocated minimal resources to prevent them from causing problems for the society's elites, but should otherwise be left to their own devices. Conversely, the most talented, intelligent and resourceful citizens should receive most of the Empire's resources (education, housing, public works, policing, etc.), as they are the ones who can be expected to contribute significantly to maintaining and advancing the Empire.

Social Darwinism may also entail *eugenics:* a policy whereby the unfit are discouraged from reproducing, encouraged to have abortions, or are simply sterilized to prevent genetic deterioration of the species. Conversely, eugenics encourages genetic elites to reproduce prodigiously, practice polygamy and be treated as "stud animals" to increase the genetic fitness of the Imperial citizenry.

While it is considered immoral in the Christian and slave moralist world to espouse Social Darwinism, in reality it is those who promote its opposite—funnelling resources toward the poor, criminal and sickly, incentivizing them to have children, taxing the elite and restricting their reproductive freedom—who are guilty of the truly immoral policies. For the ultimate arbiter of morality is not man nor some absconded god, but a pitiless, Darwinian natural law that only rewards the fit. If the slave moralists had their way, society would degenerate into a mass of shared misery, where no one of any ability who could actually drive humanity upward has any incentive to do so, and all spirit of advancement would be crushed. Indeed, life would have never risen above the slime nor humanity survived its many tribulations had such a pathological concept of morality taken root for long. Therefore the Sith, who answer to the higher morality of natural law and the Dark Side, oppose the spreaders of slave moralist poison, and espouse Social Darwinism as the best mechanism for preventing the moral, social and biological degeneration of our mankind.

THE FORCE AND THE SOURCE

The Sith believe that all life is charged with a vital energy called the Force, similar to "chi", "ki" "shakti" and "mana" in other traditions. Cultivating the Force is the key to increasing one's personal power and attaining Sith mastery. In Book III of this series, *Lords of the Force*, we described our metaphysical philosophy in terms of *the Source (Tozg), the Force (Zy), Source Systems (Tozg-Morkânz)* and *Force Orders (Zy-Gâzûlz)*. We refer you to that book for a more detailed discussion.

To recap, the Source is the formless first principle or intelligence from which our deepest values originate—a God, Brahman or Tao that has no inherent form and cannot be described in any language. The Source gives rise to *Source-forms*, which are the different forms the Source takes to different peoples which allow them to identify and interact with it—for example Jesus, the Devil, Wotan, Kali, Science, Reason or the Nation. Source-forms in turn produce a flow of Force—a metaphysical energy that expresses the "will" of the Source-form and creates passion and motivation in devotees of that form. For example, the Christian god produces *Spiritus Sancti*—the "Holy Spirit" that Christians invoke in their prayers and rituals; the Tao produces a flow of *chi*, the vital energy cultivated by Taoists; *Shakti* energy flows from the "Divine Mother" and animates the disciples of certain Hindu sects; the *Bor-Zy* (Dark Force) flows from the Black Sun and inspires Black Sunnites like Darth Imperius; the *Vi Diaboli* ("Devil Force") or "Unholy Spirit" of Satan drives Diabolists like Darth Ravenus; and so on.

A particular Source-form and Force may inspire the

Dark Side Philosophy

formation of a *Force Order (Zy-Gâzûl)*: a hierarchical lineage of Lords, Masters and Disciples of that Source-form, ranked by their Force power. Force Orders are the spiritual brotherhoods and occult lineages at the core of the world's major religions and ideologies. These Orders transmit their power and authority via Force transmission from Master to Apprentice, creating a Force lineage. For example, in Sufism, the mystical Islamic tradition, the Source-form is the god *Allah*, the Force is the divine energy called *Baraka*, the Masters of the lineage are called *Murshids* and the Lord is called the *Sheikh*. This Force Order believes its chain of transmission of Force empowerment goes back to the prophet of Islam himself, Muhammad.

The Sith Force Order, the primary focus of this book, calls its Source the *Dark Side*: a thoughtform that bestows unlimited Force power on those who know how to connect to it. This Force power manifests particularly as an intense craving for power on all levels—individual, collective, mental, physical, metaphysical, ideological and political.

THE POWER OF THE DARK SIDE

> "Only this have I learned so far, that man needs what is most evil in him for what is best in him—that whatever is most evil is his best power and the hardest stone for the highest creator; and that man must become better and more evil." —Friedrich Nietzsche

Pillar Four asserts that to maximize his power, man must learn to embrace his Shadow-mind and awaken all aspects of his nature. Man's dark side can be his most potent ally, but only if it is brought under control with Sith discipline.

All dark side psychology, endarkened philosophy and black

magick speak of the power of *the Shadow*: the dark side of human nature and the cosmos, which most try to ignore, suppress or vilify as "evil". The Sith, like the endarkened psychologist, philosopher and black magician, knows what evil lurks in the hearts of men, and how much power it has. Striving to acquire this power, and to make himself psychologically whole and strong, the Sith becomes a living embodiment of his own Shadow, rather than a walking denial of it. This makes him terrifying to the Shadow-denying Lightsiders, but it also makes him very formidable. For it gives him a gravitas, confidence and commanding presence that their subconscious minds respect, though their conscious minds reject. As Sith, this is what matters most to us: the deep truth communicated by the shadow-mind, not the superficial words and abstractions of the waking mind.

The great psychologist Carl Jung was the Westerner who popularized the idea of the Shadow, and made "integrating the Shadow" central to his psychological system. As Jung said:

> "Filling the conscious mind with ideal conceptions is a characteristic of Western theosophy, but not the confrontation with the Shadow and the world of darkness. One does not become enlightened by imagining figures of light, but by making the darkness conscious. The latter procedure, however, is disagreeable and therefore not popular."

Here Jung shows an understanding of what the endarkened always knew: that real enlightenment is a process of facing the darkness, not the light. Jung also spoke of "projecting the Shadow": the common practice of projecting one's fears, hatreds and darker nature onto another person or group, and branding them "evil". This is what the Samurai of old

Japan did vis-a-vis the Ninja, for example: projected all they found most despicable, disturbing and dishonorable onto them, so that the Ninja became the living Shadows of the Samurai. And as often happens in cases of Shadow projection, the Samurai sought to wipe out the Ninja, and in so doing to wipe out the Shadow that was nothing other than their own dark side. But this is a war that they could never win.

The secret of the Siths' power is our willingness to *be* the Shadow, and to use it as a weapon by magnifying and projecting it back upon the projector. By becoming living Shadows, Shadow-projection attacks no longer work against us. The Sith essentially says to the Lightsiders of the world: "Yes, I am your worst fears come to life. Your shaming and vilification doesn't work on me. The more you project your fears upon me, the stronger I become." This understanding is vital to our kind; it is how we stay strong in the face of animosity, and how we gain power in the face of stigmatization and fear. This understanding is what we call *Shadow-mindedness (Kâmûd-hûzûk)*. As you proceed on your Path, remember this Pillar, always striving to awaken your Dark Side and thus become a more powerful being.

The Superman

> "Man is a rope stretched between the animal and the Superman—a rope over an abyss." —Friedrich Nietzsche

The Sith are in the process of breeding a new tribe or species—a conquering race that combines the ferocious spirit of the strongest beasts with the intellect and spirit of the highest men. Indeed, we seek to exceed the abilities of beasts and men, by developing powers that will elevate us to the status of demigods or even gods. This is what is meant by the *Superman*, or *Shârûk-Tog*, as we say in Borgâl.

The concept of the Superman, or *Übermensch*, was first developed philosophically by Friedrich Nietzsche in the late 19th century, as an antidote to the *Last Man* ethos of post-Christian, nihilistic, democratic, herd-like, mediocre modern man. Nietzsche's Superman would be a *value creator*, who overcomes nihilism by living according to values originating from within himself, rather than from some external source such as religion or cultural convention (thus is Nietzsche often considered the first *existentialist* philosopher). The Superman would also overcome slave morality, by asserting himself as an aristocrat and an exceptional being—the master of the herd rather than their champion or representative.

Nietzsche introduced the Superman in his poetic masterpiece *Thus Spoke Zarathustra*. In the prologue, the prophet Zarathustra comes down from his ten year-long meditations in the mountains and announces to the people of first town:

> "I teach you the Superman. Man is something that shall be overcome. What have you done to overcome him?
>
> "All beings so far have created something beyond themselves; and do you want to be the ebb of this great flood and even go back to the beasts rather than overcome man? What is the ape to man? A laughingstock or a painful embarrassment. And man shall be just that for the Superman: a laughingstock or a painful embarrassment. You have made your way from worm to man, and much in you is still worm. Once you were apes, and even now, too, man is more ape than any ape.

> "Whoever is the wisest among you is also a mere conflict and cross between plant and ghost But do I bid you become ghosts or plants?
>
> "Behold, I teach you the Superman. The Superman is the meaning of the earth. Let your will say: the Superman shall be the meaning of the earth! I beseech you, my brothers, remain faithful to the earth, and do not believe those who speak to you of otherworldly hopes! Poison-mixers are they, whether they know it or not. Despisers of life are they, decaying and poisoned themselves, of whom the earth is weary: so let them go.

Since Nietzsche's prophetic thought, there has been an explosion of interest in the Superman idea, by writers, artists, spiritual leaders and scientists with a wide range of visions. For example, Aleister Crowley promoted a magickal vision of Nietzschean Supermen, whose maxim would be: *"do what thou wilt shall be the whole of the law"*. In 1932, Crowley called for the world to be ruled by such Supermen, whose mastery of magick would give them the powers needed to solve the world's problems:

> "We are in the middle of a world crisis. It is a very good world crisis—better than any crisis we have had before—and there is no man alive with an intellect big enough to grasp the threads of the problems which confront the world today. There are two ways out of that. Either consult a superior intelligence, which Magick shows you the way of doing, or you can develop your own mind, for it has a faculty which is as superior to the intellect as the intellect is superior to the emotions. All magical operations require a very elaborate training of one kind or another, but I think the only way out is that we have got to put men in charge of this planet who are really more than men.

We must get back to the times of the prophets or we must make ourselves prophets. And we must look at world problems from a standpoint which is entirely alien to that existing at present."

As if on cue, Adolf Hitler took power in Germany the following year and presented himself as the prophet and savior of his nation. Hitler had studied the occult in his youth and been trained by known magicians. But he saw himself not as the Superman himself, but their herald; he spoke of the "new man" who would be the cruel future overlords of his Reich:

> "What will the social order of the future be like? Comrade, I will tell you. There will be a class of overlords, after them the rank and file of the party members in hierarchical order, and then the great mass of anonymous followers, servants and workers in perpetuity, and beneath them again all the conquered foreign races, the modern slaves. And over and above all these will reign a new and exalted nobility of whom I cannot speak... but of all these plans the militant members will know nothing. The new man is living amongst us now! He is here. Isn't that enough for you? I will tell you a secret. I have seen the new man. He is intrepid and cruel. I was afraid of him."

At the same time that Hitler was building his Superman regime on the ground in Europe, Indian philosopher-yogi Sri Aurobindo was pursuing a kindler, gentler vision of superhumanity at his southern Indian ashram. Aurobindo applied evolutionary thinking to the realm of mental and spiritual development, which he believed would produce the *supermind*:

> Man is a transitional being, he is not final; for in him

and high beyond him ascend the radiant degrees which climb to a divine supermanhood.

The step from man towards superman is the next approaching achievement in the earth's evolution. There lies our destiny and the liberating key to our aspiring, but troubled and limited human existence—inevitable because it is at once the intention of the inner Spirit and the logic of Nature's process. ...

The difference between man and superman will be the difference between mind and a consciousness as far beyond it as thinking mind is beyond the consciousness of plant and animal; the differentiating essence of man is mind, the differentiating essence of superman will be supermind or a divine gnosis.

Supermen have long been a favorite subject of science-fiction writers: Stapledon's *Odd John*, Van Vogt's *Slans*, Paul Atreides of "Dune", Star Trek's *Augments*, S. M. Stirling's *Draka*, and of course the *Sith* of Star Wars. Supermen have always dominated comic books—Superman, Batman, Lex Luthor, Doctor Doom, Magneto, the X-Men, Captain America, etc.,—and have conquered modern cinema, almost single-handedly keep the movie industry solvent.

Supermen are also of great interest to many scientists and technologists. *Transhumanists* seeks to build Nietzsche's rope from the animal to the Übermensch technologically, via cybernetic, genetic or pharmacological enhancements of the species, or by building artificially intelligent machines from scratch that render carbon-based life obsolete. Transhumanist ideas have become influential on many tech elites, even becoming a new religion for some of them. While the Dark Lords take a more psychological and spiritual approach to superhumanity, we don't doubt that science and technology can play an important role in this quest, and advocate for accelerated Transhumanist research.

Attributes of the Sith Superman

We cannot predict with certainty what form the Sith Superman will take in the future, so we advocate exploring many paths of mastery and seeking knowledge in a wide range of fields. We have identified nine attributes that should give the Acolyte a very strong foundation for pursuing superhumanity, which we summarize in the box below.

Nine Attributes of the Sith Superman:

- exceptional mental and psychic powers
- mastery of martial arts, yoga, running, climbing or other physical discipline(s)
- knowledge of philosophy
- knowledge of science & technology
- knowledge of occult, psychological & religious thought
- evolutionary ideology (man is in the process of becoming something greater)
- aristocratic, warrior mentality
- possession of a creative myth or long-term vision for himself and the world
- Dark Side-awareness and -mastery

Mind Power

The fictional Sith were individuals who cultivated exceptional powers of mind: they had the ability to sense the presence of other Force-powerful beings, perform "Force-chokes", read minds, dominate wills, perceive future events, visualize empires and mold reality according to their wills. And they did all this with little or no "magickal" technology such as rituals, incantations, implements or invocations of spirits. They practiced black "mental magic", using their focused thoughts, wills, intents and imaginations as weapons to defeat the Lightsiders and manifest the world they wanted. Pillar Six, which we call *Mind Power (Hûz-Râkâ)*, encompasses all of these aspects of Sith mental power.

Mind Power is the bridge between the metaphysical and the physical; between mind and matter; between the Source and the material world; it is the mental sorcery that takes the energy from Source, which we call Force, focuses and directs it to achieve one's goals. The underlying idea is that thoughts have agency; they aren't confined to some Platonic realm of ideals, as the classical philosophers imagined, but can affect reality directly when concentrated and directed toward an objective. This principle, similar to the "New Thought", "power of positive thinking" or "Law of Attraction" that have been influential over the past century, is an ancient idea found in many metaphysical systems, including Hermeticism, Yoga and primal sorcery. Mind Power may sound irrational and magickal, but it is a pillar of the Sith "faith" because we have found it to get results, even if it is not rationally clear to us why it does so.

Mind Power sits in the metaphysical chain of causation like this:

> Source (ideal) → Force (inspiration, energy) → Mind

Power (thought, language, intent) → Manifestation (material results)

To use a physical analogy, the Source is the sun, the Force is sunlight, Mind Power is a lens, and Manifestation is the fire started by the sunlight focused by that lens.

The Nine Mental Weapons

In previous books in this series, we identified nine aspects of Mind Power that we call the *Nine Mental Weapons*; they are: *power-craving, willpower, perception, intelligence, fearlessness, persuasion, imagination, formlessness* and *endarkenment*. Each of the nine Mental Weapons has an associated *mudra*, or hand position, that serves to focus the Sith disciple's awareness on that weapon so that he may hone it or employ it as needed. The Nine Mental Weapons will be described in detail in book five of this series.

Language

One of the most powerful tools of Mind Power is language. The ability to influence minds (including your own), identify those aspects of reality that are "real", manage societies and formulate thoughts, is largely a function of language. Language has an almost unlimited magical power over human minds; recall that the very first line of the monotheist's Bible reads: "In the beginning was the Word, and the Word was with God, and the Word was God." Languages such as Hebrew, Sanskrit and Arabic are considered by some to have divine power. Most "magic" is a practice of casting "spells", which are strings of words which are thought to have a metaphyscial ability to affect minds and bend reality.

Recognizing this power, the Dark Lords have constructed their own language of *Borgâl*. Borgâl is the liturgical and black magickal language that allows us to bend the Force and shape the world according to their wills. To become a Dark Lord, all Sith Academy students are required to learn Borgâl.

Note, however, that we do not confuse language *with* reality; our belief in the existence of an "unformed world" that is formless and unnameable means that there are aspects of reality that will remain forever outside the reach of any language.

MULTIVERSALISM

The Dark Lords believe that everything imaginable exists in a larger multiverse of mind. Therefore the Sith of the Galaxy Far, Far Away are real, but exist in another universe accessible only through the "third eye" of imagination. One basis for this belief was the inter-universal transmission of knowledge received from Darth Omega by our Order's founder, Darth Imperius. The experience of vividly communicating with an entity from a "fictional" universe was enough to convince him that the Galaxy Far, Far Away is a real place, even if it is physically inaccessible to us. Other experiences, by the Dark Lords and other powerful minds, have further persuaded us that imaginal worlds are real. To name one example, J. R. R. Tolkien, author of the *Lord of the Rings* trilogy, had a series of waking dreams or visions as a young man in which he saw, heard and spoke to the people and places in his novels—the elves, dwarves, hobbits, wizards, ents, Ring-wraiths, Dark Lord, Mordor, Rivendell, etc. It was as if a portal into Middle Earth had opened in his mind, and he was transcribing what he saw. As he wrote these visions down over the years, the epic of Lord of the Rings unfolded, as if he were a historian recounting events that occurred in a real place and time.

This leads us to formulate the seventh Pillar of Sithism: *Multiversalism*. Multiversalism is a kind of inverse nihilism, in which everything imaginable is thought to exist in a larger Multiverse of ideas. Multiversalism posits that the set of all mental constructs of any kind—mathematical, mythological, artistic, magical, hallucinatory, etc.—defines the largest possible multiversal reality. All the mythical gods, fictional heroes, fantasy realms, dream worlds and supernatural entities are real, they just inhabit different dimensions within the larger Multiverse of mind. Similar worldviews have been proposed by artists and mystics down through the ages, but most of them have fallen into disrepute and obscurity in the Western world since the so-called Enlightenment. But as modern physics itself embraces increasingly esoteric-sounding multiversal models, and as technology blurs the distinction between real and imaginary worlds, we foresee a new convergence of science, art and mysticism around a worldview like Multiversalism.

Multiversalism considers the rationalist project to lay down the laws of a single, objective reality futile, misguided and repugnant. The campaign of militant atheists to impose the epistemological totalitarianism of the scientific method is as delusional as Christian dogma was in Galileo's time. If some subset of humanity chooses to collectively imagine a god and worship him, and derives power from so doing, then more power to them! Every Universalist philosophy or "tyranny of the real" must be overthrown in favor of the unlimited freedom of the Multiversalist imagination. Art and magick become more important than science in a Multiversalist civilization, because while science describes the laws and limits of this universe, art and magick find ways to break them. You don't like a universal speed limit of three hundred thousand kilometers per second? Imagine a universe without one, and use technological or magickal arts to create an arbitrarily real virtual world where no such upper bound exists. The final frontier of the Multiverse is therefore not the three lawful dimensions of outer space, but the infinite-dimensional creative chaos of inner space.

Finally, we speculate that the Multiverse of ideas is identical to consciousness itself. All of reality springs from consciousness. Everything we are conscious of is real. The mind and the Multiverse are therefore one and the same. It seems to us that the pre-scientific mystics had it right all along: reality is a mental construct created and explored by the technology of the imagination.

Galactic Empire

For the Sith, the cosmos is a call to greatness and a place to acquire unlimited power. The primary exoteric goal of the Sith is to drive civilization toward ever-higher levels of organization and power—to establish global, solar and galactic Empires under Dark Side rule.

But the Empire is not just a political project; it is a symbol of a lust for greatness in all aspects of individual and collective life. The desire to be an Empire-builder, and a citizen of the Empire, reflects the longing to be part of a civilization that seeks and glorifies power in all its forms. This longing wells up from the Shadow-mind; it is not something that can or needs to be rationally explained. One feels the Empire as a profound, inspiring vision—the expression in the macrocosm of a drive for power and greatness welling up from the microcosm. This drive lays dormant in every human being, though it is often deeply buried by layers of social conditioning and demoralizing life experience. Our task as Sith Imperial heralds is to awaken this latent longing in other beings; to light a fire in their souls with visions of greatness that becomes a mighty conflagration that consumes the universe.

Formlessness

> "I must state that Zithodûn, the way of the Sith, makes its way, running towards a great void. If you ask what Zithodûn is, the answer is it has no shape. If Zithodûn is sought for, it has no heart. Just try to see and realize clearly the way of your own shadow-mind." —Darth Imperius (paraphrasing Natori Masatake)

> "Be extremely subtle, even to the point of formlessness. Be extremely mysterious, even to the point of soundlessness. Thereby you can be the director of the opponent's fate." —Sun Tzu

The Sith who has no fixed form, who cannot be seen, heard or even suspected, is the most dangerous Sith of all. The Sith who works his will invisibly, becoming a force of nature like the wind, is the most powerful type of being. This is the highest state of Sith mastery: never drawing attention to yourself, never leaving calling-cards, always changing your outer form, making every operation look like an accident or an act of the gods. The Sith who wishes to endure will follow this advice. Flashy personalities burn brightly but soon flame out; rigid organizations cannot adapt to change and soon fail; but subtle, formless power that stays in the shadows and adapts to any eventuality can survive forever.

It is said that the greatest trick the Devil ever pulled is to convince the world he doesn't exist. The same is true of the Sith, who have been called devils for similar reasons. For both the Devil and Sith know this to be true: only power that is hidden is power that endures. Be as formless and nameless as the Dark Tao itself, and none can deny or destroy you.

In 1938, the influential Zen teacher D. T. Suzuki wrote the following about his religion:

> Zen has no special doctrine or philosophy, no set of concepts or intellectual formulas, except that it tries to release one from the bondage of birth and death, by means of certain intuitive modes of understanding peculiar to itself. It is, therefore, extremely flexible in adapting itself to almost any philosophy and moral doctrine as long as its intuitive teaching is not interfered with. It may be found wedded to anarchism or fascism, communism or democracy, atheism or idealism, or any political or economic dogmatism. It is, however, generally animated with a certain revolutionary spirit, and when things come to a deadlock—as they do when we are overloaded with conventionalism, formalism, and other cognate isms— Zen asserts itself and proves to be a destructive force.

If we replace the word "Zen" in the above quote with the word "Sithism", and say that it "seeks unlimited power and immortality" instead of "tries to release one from the bondage of birth and death", we are not far from our conception of the Sith Path. While we may prefer certain philosophical and political forms, finding them more congenial to our spirit or susceptible to our influence, a true Sith Lord can work within any ideological milieu and co-opt it for his own ends. For Sithism, like Zen, is a path of intuition and flexibility rather than rigid adherence to dogma. We are concerned with the inner nature of individuals, with their Dark Side power and perception, and understand that powerful beings can be found at the top of any social system.

If a given society requires us to adopt a Light Side persona to accumulate power or infiltrate a regime in order to topple it from within, then that is the form we will adopt. But inwardly, the Sith should remain formless, and gain our most insidious strength from this quality of *formlessness*, or *chanbrânûk*. For the Dark Side, like the shadows, has no inherent form, but only takes temporary forms depending on the nature of the light that is cast upon it. By staying as fluid as the Darkness, the Sith Lord can hide in plain sight, gathering formless, invisible power. This principle is the ninth Pillar of Sithism.

A SURVEY OF PHILOSOPHY

In this chapter we shall survey the field of philosophy from a Sith perspective, discussing various schools of thought that have influenced our worldview or are otherwise relevant to our project. The educated Sith philosopher should be familiar with the major ideas and writings discussed in this chapter. In the war of ideas that is philosophy, this material will ensure that you are armed for battle!

Key Philosophies

Nietzscheism

The work of Friedrich Nietzsche constitutes a uniquely inspired and potent body of thought that has influenced Sith philosophy more than any other Western source. We consider Nietzsche the prophet of the Dark Side in the Western world—a man whose anti-rationalist, Romantic-Satanic philosophizing at the peak of Enlightenment triumphalism shook European philosophy to its foundations.

The main tenets of Nietzschean philosophy include the following:

- The "Will to Power" is the source of man's highest values and meaning. All life, and even inanimate matter, is driven by this primal urge.

- "Evil" is essential to the achievement of greatness. All great things will be called "evil" by the guardians of a mediocre status quo.

- Judaism and Christianity are the source of "slave moralism": the spirit of guilt-mongering and glorification of the weak that overthrew the aristocratic values of the Classical world.

- Man is not an end, but a bridge between the animal and the *Superman*—the value-creating aristocrat who has overcome slave moralism and nihilism and seeks greatness.

- Modern civilization is in the age of the *Last Man*—comfort-seeking, democratic, utilitarian, nihilistic, effeminate, un-heroic cowards who hold no great ideas worth fighting for.

One indication of the potency of Nietzsche's thought is the wildly diverging groups he has inspired: left-wingers and right-wingers, postmodernists and reactionaries, capitalists and communists, monarchists and anarchists, secular humanists and mystics, scientists and magicians, atheists, Hindus, Muslims, Nazis, Jews, and even a few Christians.

Taoism

Of all the philosophies they have studied to date, the Dark Lords have found none more profound than Taoism. Taoism posits a primordial *Tao*, or *Way*, which is the ultimate, formless principle underlying all phenomena. The Tao gives rise to *yin* and *yang*—two poles which together produce all other phenomena. Light and dark, heat and cold and ugliness and beauty are examples of yin-yang polarities; they give rise to each other and cannot exist without each other. The Tao is spoken of in terms of paradoxes—constant but ever-changing, attaining heights by seeking the depths, accumulating wealth by giving everything away, achieving everything by doing nothing, growing wiser by forgetting what one has learned, etc. Essentially, Taoism posits a balanced universe: nothing can never be entirely "black" or "white"; everything contains the seeds of its own destruction; the harder you push in one direction the more you bring about its opposite.

As a religious tradition, Taoism contains numerous sects and lineages, which follow a master-apprentice methodology not unlike our own Force Order. In their spiritual practice, Taoists focus on the cultivation of *chi*—the universal vital energy that flows according to the Tao. They have developed elaborate techniques of inner alchemy, meditation, yoga, martial arts and medicine to enhance their chi and attain long life. According to their legends, the greatest Taoists masters have achieved superhuman lifespans and physical feats through extremely rigorous training, and this practice continues to this day. Taoist adepts are also known to pursue one side of the yin-yang duality exclusively in order achieve heightened states of energy and Tao-awareness. All in all, we find in Taoism a profound tradition that mirrors our own vision in many respects. That we sometimes call our own path "Dark Taoism" shows the great regard we have for this philosophy and way of life.

Traditionalism

Traditionalism is a school of thought developed primarily by European intellectuals in the 20th century as a reaction to the revolutionizing and disorienting effects of modernity. Traditionalists seek to re-connect to those primal currents of philosophy and spirituality that they believe all great pre-modern civilizations had in common—the "perennial wisdom" of universal, eternal metaphysical truths. The emphasis of Traditionalism is on the restoration of perennial metaphysics to its rightful place as the guiding philosophy for society, rather being discarded as a useless relic of an unenlightened age. Major exponents of Traditionalism include René Guénon, Frithjof Schuon, Julius Evola, Hossein Nasr and Huston Smith.

The most Sithy of the Traditionalists, and the most interesting to us, is Julius Evola. A profound esotericist and one-time fascist theoretician, Evola celebrates the aristocratic, ascetic warrior-mystic as the epitome of the Traditional man, and harshly criticizes the sort of modern "progressive" man who accumulates material wealth and seeks pleasure while growing ever more degenerate, dependent, effeminate, pacifistic and spiritually empty. Evola points to the Hindu caste system, European feudalism and Imperial Japan as examples of traditionally ordered societies that produce men of strength and nobility. In such societies there is a divine order, in which authority flows from *the Source* (Brahma, God, etc.) downward to the monarchs, nobles, priests, warriors, workers and merchants in a strict hierarchy. Modernity, in this view, has been a process of undoing or inverting the traditional order, such that now, in place of rule by warrior-kings and priests, we have a regime dominated by merchants and technocrats who have no sense of a divine order, no conception of metaphysics and no vision beyond base materialism and hedonism.

Our project of Sithism, while being in some respects radically post-modern and revolutionary, also incorporates strong elements of Traditionalist thought. For the *Empire* is very similar to the Traditionalist vision of a sacred imperium: there is a "divine" or metaphysical hierarchy, in which power flows downward from the Source, to the Emperor, the Dark Lords, Apprentices, Acolytes and into the larger society; the authority of the rulers is absolute, being based on Force power rather than legal documents; the method of governance is magocracy, in which the rulers are magicians who employ symbols, rituals, mental projections and metaphysical constructs to assert their rule more than rationalist abstractions or brute force; the focus is on long-term stability and achievement of great projects rather than solving short-term problems driven by populist sentiment; the doctrines of democracy, materialism and utilitarianism that form the basis of modern states are discarded in favor of magocracy, panpsychism and romanticism.

In our view, such a civilization, which incorporates traditional metaphysics into a postmodern, scientific culture, holds the cure for the "Force starvation crisis" that we wrote about previously in **Lords of the Force**, and which is literally destroying the bodies, minds and souls of the men of this age. Traditionalism is an important philosophical strand in the web we must weave to break the spell of the Light Side orders and prepare minds for the coming of the Empire.

Zen

Zen Buddhism has been a major influence on the thinking and mentality of Darth Imperius, the seminal mind behind the Sith Academy project. Here are four aspects of Zen philosophy and practice that he has found particularly useful on his path of power:

Meditation. Zen is essentially the practice of sitting meditation; any philosophy of Zen is secondary to this activity. The power of Zen meditation to clear the mind of mental chatter and useless concepts, focus attention, sharpen the "sword of Will", and return awareness to the present moment and environment, is something we strongly encourage all Acolytes to develop.

Formlessness. The Zen doctrine of *Shunyata*—that there is a formless void underlying all phenomena—is an idea we find intuitively compelling and correct. We have incorporated this doctrine into the ninth Pilllar of Sithism, Formlessness, as previously discussed.

Will and Intuition. Zen encourages the development of willpower and intuition over analytic thought and moralism —the two favored modes of Western Light Side thinkers. Through Zen practice, one develops a resolute will which proceeds immediately towards an objective without analysis or guilt. This has made Zen popular with warriors over the centuries; as Dark Side warriors, every Sith can profit from it as well.

Stoicism and Asceticism. Zen, like other forms of Buddhism, encourages a mentality of stoic acceptance of reality, endurance of hardship and rejection of attachment to the desires of the flesh. A Sith need not accept any of these doctrines on principle, but can gain significant inner strength and independence of mind by practicing them when needed nonetheless.

Satanism

One of most notable attempts to formulate a coherent Dark Side philosophy is the philosophy of *Satanism*, as expounded by Anton LaVey and others since the 1960s.

Satanism propounds a philosophy of militant self-interest, vitalism, materialism and hedonism; it rejects traditional monotheistic virtues such as guilt, chastity, submission to God, collectivism, charity for the undeserving, turning the other cheek, otherworldliness and mystical "pipe dreams". LaVey's Satanism is essentially radical individualism and hedonism, overlaid with a theatrical occult and artistic style. It has clear echoes of Friedrich Nietzsche's anti-Christian, pro-"Superman" philosophy, Aleister Crowley's sacrireligious showmanship, and Ayn Rand's celebration of selfishness and individual greatness. LaVey himself characterized his ideology as "just Ayn Rand's philosophy with ceremony and ritual added". Satanism was a noteworthy attempt to popularize Nietzschean and Randian philosophy and offer an alternative to both traditional monotheism and the "hippie" or New Age ethos of the so-called "counter-culture". LaVey's genius was realizing that the modern world was tailor-made by Satan; that the American ethos of capitalism, individualism and "life, liberty and pursuit of happiness" are perfectly compatible with his brand of Satanic philosophy— much more so than Christianity. The fact that this philosophy is largely mainstream today suggests that it has been rather successful in influencing society, or at least in being ahead of the curve in anticipating its trajectory. LaVey's declaration of 1966 as "Year One of the Satanic Age" looks rather accurate in retrospect, as it does seem to these writers that there was a pronounced cultural shift in the Satanic direction starting around that date.

The Dark Lords respect the philosophical black magick that LaVey has worked on this society, but we have some significant disagreements with his philosophy of Satanism. For one, we do not agree with its Randian rejection of mysticism as mere "pipe dreams". For us, mysticism is a means of exploring the shadow-mind and the dark or occulted aspects of reality, in an effort to unlock knowledge and powers that are held in check by the conscious, rational mind. LaVey himself seemed to understand this at times, such as when he described Satan as "the dark force in nature", and engaged in ritualistic and artistic work that was clearly an expression of his own shadow-mind. But

Satanism, particularly post-LaVey, has become associated with a rather mundane materialism, rationalism and atheism that we do no subscribe to. For our kind, Satanism means black magick and dark forces beyond reason, which can never be reduced to any mundane ideology.

Secondly, we are not opposed to collectivism in principle, as are Ayn Rand, LaVeyan Satanists and other disciples of the Left Hand Path. We have no problem with cults, armies and empires who choose to march collectively under the banner of black magicians; indeed, this is one of our primary projects as Dark Lords. To reduce humanity to atomized individuals pursuing a lifestyle of "sex, drugs and rock & roll" is to us rather cretinous, as it negates the immense potential for power and glory that exists in collectives led by inspired and truly Satanic individuals.

To rectify these and other shortcomings of LaVey's Satanism and offer a potent alternative, the Dark Lords created the *Temple of Satan*—an organization that propounds a truly Satanic philosophy of Devil-worship, glorification of "evil", breeding of the Antichrist, real black magick and demonolatry, collective militant action and world domination. For more information about this organization and its philosophy, see our book ***Temple of Satan: Pact With the Devil***.

Chaoism

Chaoism is a philosophy associated with Peter J. Carroll and other proponents of *chaos magick*. Chaoism is a sorcerer's creed; it is less concerned with the ultimate nature of reality than with getting results within that reality by any means, without regard for the limits of any tradition, culture or religion. Chaotes maintain that belief itself is the source of magickal power, regardless of its nature or "objective truth". A Chaote may invoke any belief system, mythology or fictional story (even Star Wars characters!) to work his magick if it inspires his imagination and will. Chaoism itself borrows from many other philosophies, including shamanism, Taoism, Tantrism, postmodernism and the fictional metaphysics of H. P. Lovecraft and Michael Moorcock, which feature worlds metaphysically torn between the forces of Order and Chaos. Chaotes maintain that we are at the dawn of the "fifth aeon", or age of consciousness, which follows the preceding Shamanic, Pagan, Monotheist and Atheist Aeons. This new aeon is the aeon of Chaoism, which is a return to shamanism but in a higher form.

In his seminal book on chaos magick, *Liber Null*, Peter Carroll makes the following prophetic prediction:

> Decades, possibly centuries, of warfare lie ahead. The remnants of monotheism are collapsing fast, despite the odd revival, before secular humanism and consumerism. The technological, atheist super-states are trying for a stranglehold on human consciousness. We are entering a phase which may become as oppressive to the spirit as medieval monotheism. The production/consumption equation is becoming increasingly difficult to grasp or balance as the consumer religion of the masses begins to dictate politics.
>
> More and more mechanisms for the forceful regulation of behavior have to be introduced as population density pushes individuals to seek ever more bizarre forms of satisfaction in material sensationalism. ...
>
> The blind logic of technology and consumerism will cause alienation, disaffection, greed, and identity crisis

to rise to such catastrophic levels that the situation may explode into a very destructive war. There may be a breakdown of society which may take the form of an anti-technological jihad. These will not resolve the contradictions of the system but merely introduce a new dark age and slow the changes down. However momentous these events may seem, if they happen, they will not affect the movement of consciousness in the long run. They will only affect its timing. But the Illuminati must be ready to exploit the changes which will definitely occur.

Carroll predicts these changes will include the death of spirituality, superstition, identity, belief and ideology. In effect, Carroll is prophesying the wholesale dissolution of the philosophical structures of the past six thousand years and the onset of an age of chaos, which will then bring forth a new shamanic age of expanded consciousness and possibilities. This is reminiscent of Hindu metaphysics, according to which we are in the *Kali Yuga*—the final world age of the four-age cycle, which is marked by devolution, dissolution and chaos before the onset of the next *Satya Yuga*, or Golden Age. Here Chaoism overlaps not only with Hinduism, but with the Traditionalism of Guenon, Evola and others. In fact there are a number modern thinkers, such as the Russian Alexander Dugin, who have combined the two currents, positing that chaos magick can accelerate the dissolution of the present age of degeneration and bring about a new age of traditional virtues. This type of Chaoism may have played a significant role in recent political developments, as the online "meme magick" of supporters of Donald Trump, the influence of his Traditionalist-informed advisors and Russian Duginite memetic machinations may all have combined to put their "Chaos Lord" and "troll-in-chief" in the White House!

It should be apparent to the astute reader that the Dark Lords have been strongly influenced by Chaoism, and are themselves working powerful chaos magick with their evocation of the Sith current on this planet and their creation of an Order inspired by a cult from popular fiction that seeks to conquer this world. And this is just one of many metaphysical currents they have pursued using the philosophy and methods of Chaoism.

Recommended Reading

The following are some writings that we recommend every student of Sith philosophy read and reflect upon.

Metaphysics

Tao Te Ching by Lao Tzu
Metaphysics by Aristotle
Corpus Hermeticum by Hermes Trismegistus
Philosophy of the Unconscious by Eduard von Hartmann
Synchronicity: An Acausal Connecting Principle by Carl Jung

Philosophy of Power

The Will to Power by Friedrich Nietzsche
On Power by Bertrand de Jouvenel
The Lucifer Principle by Howard Bloom

Political Philosophy

Dialogues by Plato
The Prince by Machiavelli
Reflections on Violence by George Sorel
The Doctrine of Fascism by Benito Mussolini
Mein Kampf by Adolf Hitler

Milestones by Sayeed Qutb
A Primer of Politics by James Combs

Warrior Philosophy

The Book of Five Rings by Miyamoto Musashi
Shoninki by Natori Masatake
The Art of War by Sun Tzu
Metaphysics of War by Julius Evola

Eastern Spirituality

The Three Pillars of Zen by Philip Kapleau
Zen at War by Brian Victoria
Zen and Japanese Culture by D. T. Suzuki
The Tibetan Book of the Dead by Walter Evans-Wentz
The Yoga of Power by Julius Evola

Superman Philosophy

Man into Superman by R.C.W. Ettinger
The Future Evolution of Man by Sri Aurobindo
Thus Spake Zarathustra by Friedrich Nietzsche

Philosophy of Morality & Religion

The Antichrist by Friedrich Nietzsche
On the Geneology of Morals by Friedrich Nietzsche
Might is Right by Ragnar Redbeard
The Satanic Bible by Anton Szandor LaVey

Magickal Philosophy

Transcendental Magic, its Doctrine and Ritual by Éliphas Lévi
Magick in Theory and Practice by Aleister Crowley
The Black Arts by Richard Cavendish

Liber Null & Psychonaut by Peter Carroll

Philosophy of Mind & Psychonautics

The Doors of Perception by Aldous Huxley
The Deep Self by John C. Lily
Simulations of God: The Science of Belief by John C. Lily

Traditionalism

Revolt Against the Modern World, by Julius Evola
The Reign of Quantity and the Signs of the Times by René Guénon

Galactic Imperialism

Dune by Frank Herbert
The Overview Effect by Frank White
The Foundation Trilogy by Isaac Asimov
The Darth Bane Trilogy by Drew Karpyshyn
The Millennial Project: Colonizing the Galaxy in Eight Easy Steps by Marshall Savage

Esoteric & Philosophical Fiction

The Third Eye (and subsequent novels) by Lobsang Rampa
Don Juan: A Yaqui Way of Knowledge (and subsequent novels) by Carlos Castaneda
Opening the Dragon Gate: The Making of a Modern Taoist Wizard by Chen Kaiguo

ECHELON FOUR DOCTRINE

In *The Path of Power* we give an overview of *The Nine Echelons of Sith Mastery*—the training doctrine of the Sith Order. Here we describe the fourth Pillar, Maxim and Canon, as well as the Echelon Four Challenges that the Acolyte must complete to advanced to the next level in the Order.

Echelon Four Precepts

Pillar Four: The Power of the Dark Side

> *"Man needs what is most evil in him for what is best in him."* To maximize his power, man must learn to embrace his shadow-mind (kâmûd-hûz) and awaken all aspects of his nature. Man's dark side can be his most potent ally, but only if it is brought under control with Sith discipline.

Pillar Four has already been discussed in the "Nine Pillars of Sithism" chapter of this book.

Maxim Four: Patience, Cunning and Secrecy

> *I will be patient, cunning, and secretive in my quest for power.*

Maxim Four is key to the Sith Lord's quest, individually and as an Order. For the Sith Path is by nature the most dangerous and threatening path one can walk; this means it will provoke strong reactions from Light Side forces, who may consider us "too dangerous to be left alive". As a matter of survival and strategy, our kind must operate in the shadows, waiting, covertly plotting and machinating until the time is right to strike.

There is a powerful expression of this Maxim in the words of the legendary Sith Lord Darth Nihl, who told Darth Havok after the Sith were defeated and scattered by the Jedi:

> "We will disperse into the galaxy in small numbers, masking ourselves, hiding amidst the enemy. We will infiltrate governments on every planet. All must be brought down for something new to be created. Together or alone, we will slip onto worlds and strike from the shadows. We will be invisible. We will be patient. All that exists will be torn apart from within. Darth Krayt's vision of the galaxy remade will be realized. He lives in us. The Sith will prevail."

Wise words for all Sith to remember, and live by!

Canon Four: Apprenticeship

> *I understand that to become a Dark Lord, I must become an Apprentice of one of the Ruling Two and pass his final trials.*

Canon Four codifies the importance of the Master-Apprentice relationship for our Order, and of trials and testing for determining worthiness for Dark Lordship. Only by personal interaction with a Dark Lord can the Force transmission be achieved that ensures the Dark Lord lineage is preserved, and the Apprentice proves his Dark Side power. This Apprenticeship may take years, and result in death of one's Master—the ultimate proof of one's faith in our path.

Philosophy Quotes

"The Sith are not placid stars but singularities. Rather than burn with a muted purpose, we warp space and time to twist the galaxy to our own design." —Darth Plagueis

"Light will for a time have to be called darkness: this is the path you must tread." —Friedrich Nietzsche, *Human, All Too Human*

"Do you want a name for this world? A solution for all of its riddles? A light for you, too, you best-concealed, strongest, most intrepid, most midnightly men?— This world is the will to power—and nothing besides! And you yourselves are also this will to power—and nothing besides!" —Friedrich Nietzsche, *The Will to Power*

"The struggle between good and evil is the primal disease of the mind." —Chan Master Seng-Ts'an

"Zen has no special doctrine or philosophy, no set of concepts or intellectual formulas, except that it tries to release one from the bondage of birth and death, by means of certain intuitive modes of understanding peculiar to itself. It is, therefore, extremely flexible in adapting itself to almost any philosophy and moral doctrine as long as its intuitive teaching is not interfered with. It may be found wedded to anarchism or fascism, communism or democracy, atheism or idealism, or any political or economic dogmatism. It is, however, generally animated with a certain revolutionary spirit, and when things come to a deadlock—as they do when we are overloaded with conventionalism, formalism, and other cognate isms—Zen asserts itself and proves to be a destructive force." —D. T. Suzuki, *Zen and Japanese Culture*

"All human thought, all science, all religion, is the holding of a candle to the night of the universe." —Clark Ashton Smith

---

"We will glorify war—the world's only hygiene—militarism, patriotism, the destructive gesture of freedom bringers, beautiful ideas worth dying for, and scorn for woman. We will destroy the museums, libraries, academies of every kind, we will fight moralism, feminism, every opportunistic or utilitarian cowardice." —F. T. Marinetti, *Futurist Manifesto*

"Fascism, the more it considers and observes the future and the development of humanity quite apart from political considerations of the moment, believes neither in the possibility nor the utility of perpetual peace. It thus repudiates the doctrine of Pacifism—born of a renunciation of the struggle and an act of cowardice in the face of sacrifice. War alone brings up to its highest tension all human energy and puts the stamp of nobility upon the peoples who have courage to meet it." —Benito Mussolini, *The Doctrine of Fascism*

"Liberty is exhausted. Man must seek new strength in his black basic nature. I say it, an intellectual, the eternal libertarian." —Pierre Drieu La Rochelle, *Socialisme Fasciste*

"When a man embarks on the paths of sorcery he becomes aware, in a gradual manner, that ordinary life has been forever left behind; that knowledge is indeed a frightening affair; that the means of the ordinary world are no longer a buffer for him; and that he must adopt a new way of life if he is going to survive. The first thing he ought to do, at that point, is to want to become a warrior. The frightening nature of knowledge leaves one no alternative but to become a warrior." —Carlos Castaneda, *The Teachings of Don Juan*

"I consider the positions of kings and rulers as that of dust motes. I observe treasure of gold and gems as so many bricks and pebbles. I look upon the finest silken robes as tattered rags. I see myriad worlds of the universe as small seeds of fruit, and the greatest lake in India as a drop of oil on my foot. I perceive the teachings of the world to be the illusion of magicians. I discern the highest conception of emancipation as golden brocade in a dream, and view the holy path of the illuminated one as flowers appearing in one's eyes. I see meditation as a pillar of a mountain, Nirvana as a nightmare of daytime. I look upon the judgment of right and wrong as the serpentine dance of a dragon, and the rise and fall of beliefs as but traces left by the four seasons." —Gautama Buddha

"Death is not an event in life: we do not live to experience death. If we take eternity to mean not infinite temporal duration but timelessness, then eternal life belongs to those who live in the present. Our life has no end in the way in which our visual field has no limits." —Ludwig Wittgenstein

"Thinking begins only when we have come to know that reason, glorified for centuries, is the stiff-necked adversary of thought."

"If I take death into my life, acknowledge it, and face it squarely, I will free myself from the anxiety of death and the pettiness of life—and only then will I be free to become myself."

"When the farthest corner of the globe has been conquered technologically and can be exploited economically; when any incident you like, in any place you like, at any time you like, becomes accessible as fast as you like; when you can simultaneously "experience" an assassination attempt against a king in France and a symphony concert in Tokyo; when time is nothing but speed, instantaneity, and simultaneity, and time as history has vanished from all Being of all peoples; when a boxer counts as the great man of a people; when the tallies of millions at mass meetings are a triumph; then, yes then, there still looms like a specter over all this uproar the question: what for? — where to? — and what then?"

—Martin Heidegger

Philosophy Praxis

In the Sith black magickal worldview, thoughts are things, which means that philosophy is not an exercise in impotent abstraction, but in distilling powerful thoughts into actionable ideas. Sith philosophizing is a process of focusing, clarifying and intensifying one's thought so as to transform the mind into a potent tool, much as a laser drill focuses light in order to cut through steel or a forge turns raw metal into a killing blade. Below we describe a few practices that we recommend for the Sith philosopher, to sharpen his thinking and get maximum cutting power from his mind.

Thought-Sanctum

> "Here in my meditation chamber I can see the galaxy in my mind's eye; I can visualize vast armies, powerful fleets, invincible warriors—and with Sith arts, my imagination can make them real!" —Naga Sadow

In the Star Wars universe, Sith Lords often had meditation chambers where they meditated, mentated and schemed. The Sith philosopher in this universe should establish a similar space, which we call a *thought-sanctum (kurzât-kyârtan)*, where he can meditate and focus his thoughts without distractions. We have previously instructed the Acolyte to establish a *râkâdwân ("power space")*; the thought-sanctum may be the same space, or it may be a place that is specifically designed for undisturbed thinking. The thought-sanctum is not a magickal ritual chamber, so it need not have any symbols, adornments, altars, ritual items and the like. You enter your thought-sanctum only to think, read, write or engage in various mental exercises; the more minimal you keep it the better.

A simple sanctum could be a small room with only a cushion or chair. Or you could build a special chamber which encloses you like Darth Vader's meditation chamber, giving you total quiet and privacy. If you can find a private cave or tunnel, that is excellent. Leave electronic devices outside your sanctum; take books for reading or paper for writing if you require them, but leave phones, tablets and computers outside so you will not be distracted by phone calls, messages, apps or web sites. One of the purposes of a thought-sanctum is to separate yourself from the matrix of technological distractions that has engulfed and addled modern man, making it difficult for him to meditate deeply on any subject. Follow the example of illuminated minds who have left a lasting imprint of their thought upon the world after extended meditation in sanctums—such as the Buddha under the Bodhi tree or Bodhidharma and Muhammad in their caves.

Library

A Dark Lord reading in his library

Books are some of the most potent doorways into larger worlds of thought and domains of intellectual power. A library is to a Sith philosopher as an arsenal is to a general: a storage place for an array of potent intellectual weapons. Every aspiring Dark Lord should therefore begin amassing a library of important texts relevant to our philosophy and our path at the earliest opportunity. Acquire hardcover books and put them in high quality bookcases; do not be cheap in building your library, as you value a thing only as much as you pay for it. Decorate your library with artifacts that inspire you on your path of knowledge, such as black candles, banners, weapons and skulls. In time, a Dark Side library will become a concentrated source of black magickal energy, as the stored knowledge and mental energy you expend there combine to produce a potent nexus of intellectual power.

Don't make the uneducated Aspirant's mistake of only acquiring books on a narrow range of topics that only appeal to your present interests and state of mind. Acquire books on a wide range of subjects, including philosophy, religion, occultism, literature, history, politics, physical science and psychology, written from Dark Side and Light Side perspectives alike. Find powerful minds from any tradition or culture and add their "thought-bombs" to your arsenal. For some suggested reading material to add to your library, see the "Recommended Reading" list elsewhere in this book.

Echelon Four Challenges

Challenge #1: Thought-Sanctum

Establish a thought-sanctum as described above. Begin using the sanctum every day for at least one hour. After at least 14 days of regular use, write a report about the experience. Describe the sanctum in detail, providing pictures if desired. What significant ideas or insights did you have in your sanctum? What did you read or write? Do you find your sanctum empowering? How might it be improved?

Challenges #2-3: Philosophy Readings

Choose two books listed under "Recommended Reading" in the "A Survey of Philosophy" chapter of this book. Discuss each book in an essay of at least 600 words. Be sure to address the following questions for both books:

1) What are the main philosophical arguments or tenets presented in the book?

2) In what ways does the book add to or change your thinking with respect to Dark Side philosophy?

3) Discuss any major disagreements you have with the book's ideas.

4) Discuss anything else about the book that you find significant.

Challenge #4: Your Philosophy of Power

Based on your own reflections, readings and experiences, describe your personal philosophy of power. What is power? Is it primarily personal, metaphysical, political, cosmic or something else? Why is power important to you? How will you acquire more of it? Write down your thoughts in an essay of at least 600 words.

Challenge #5: Your Metaphysical Philosophy

Review the metaphysical ideas discussed in the "Metaphysics" chapter of this book. Critique anything you strongly disagree with, and offer some of your own ideas. What are some of your basic metaphysical beliefs or theories? How do these ideas affect how you live your life or view the world? Write down your thoughts in an essay of at least 600 words.

Challenge #6: Death Meditations

Begin a daily practice of death meditations, as described in the "Way of Samurai" section of the "Philosophy of Death" chapter. Every day in your thought-sanctum, meditate for at least 20 minutes on your death. Visualize yourself dying in various ways—being killed violently by a bullet or a blade; dying in a car accident or plane crash; being hung, poisoned or killed in an electric chair, having a heart attack; succumbing to disease, etc. Imagine the process in detail—

how it feels physically, your thoughts and emotions as it occurs, how others react, etc.

After at least nine days of daily death meditations, reflect on your philosophy of life and death. What is the significance of death to you? In what ways does awareness of death change how you live? Do you seek to defeat it scientifically, transcend it mystically, live with it existentially, worship it, or something else? Write down your thoughts in an essay of at least 600 words.

Challenge #7: Your Political Philosophy

Review the political philosophies discussed in the "Political Philosophy" chapter of this book. Describe your preferred political philosophy. Is it one of the ruling systems described, or something else? Why do you prefer your chosen system? How are you pursuing the realization of that system in the world, and how do you intend to do so? Write down your thoughts in an essay of at least 600 words.

Challenge #8: Your Cosmic Philosophy

Review the four cosmic schools discussed in the "Cosmic Philosophy" chapter of this book. Which of the four schools do you most strongly identify with, and why? How does this philosophy inform your path to Dark Lordship? Is there a school of thought besides these four that you prefer? If so, describe it. Write down your thoughts in an essay of at least 600 words.

Challenge #9: The Nine Pillars of Sithism

Discuss the Nine Pillars of Sithism presented in this book. Are there any you disagree with, or other Pillars you feel should be added? How are the Pillars empowering to you? Write down your thoughts in an essay of at least 600 words.

EPILOGUE

This concludes our writings related to Dark Side philosophy and Echelon Four training to date.

To continue your journey to Dark Lordship, acquire the next book in the *Nine Echelons of Sith Mastery* series—***Shadows of the Mind***—where we will explore "mind tricks", mental magick and the unlimited powers of the Shadow-mind. *Shadows of the Mind* is coming soon from Sith Academy Publications. The Dark Lords will be waiting for you. Râk âm chod!

-The Dark Lords-

Imperial Year 8, Month 1 (September, 2018)

CORRESPONDENCE

The Dark Lords occasionally send out books from their library at no cost or otherwise correspond with individuals who make an offering to the Black Temple. To be considered for a free book, mail a dark gift along with a hand-written letter telling us more about yourself to the address below. Be sure to tell us which book you are interested in.

SA
3102 Hoyt Ave #5361
Everett, WA 98206

Râk âm chod!

CORRESPONDENCE

Made in the USA
Monee, IL
19 January 2024